HOW TO BE YOUR OWN CONTRACTOR

HOW TO BE YOUR OWN CONTRACTOR

Gene and Katie Hamilton

COLLIER BOOKS

Macmillan Publishing Company • New York

Maxwell Macmillan Canada • Toronto

Maxwell Macmillan International
New York • Oxford • Singapore • Sydney

Collier Books
Macmillan Publishing Company
866 Third Avenue, New York, NY 10022

Maxwell Macmillan Canada, Inc.
1200 Eglinton Avenue East, Suite 200
Don Mills, Ontario M3C 3N1

Macmillan Publishing Company is part of the Maxwell Communication Group of Companies.

Library of Congress Cataloging-in-Publication Data
Hamilton, Gene.
How to be your own contractor / Gene and Katie Hamilton.—1st Collier Books ed.
p.   cm.
Includes index.
ISBN 0-02-033210-6
1. Dwellings—Remodeling—Amateurs' manuals. 2. House construction—Amateurs' manuals. 3. Contractors. I. Hamilton, Katie. II. Title.
TH4816.H287   1991
692'.8—dc20   90-22259   CIP

Macmillan books are available at special discounts for bulk purchases for sales promotions, premiums, fund-raising, or educational use. For details, contact:

Special Sales Director
Macmillan Publishing Company
866 Third Avenue
New York, NY 10022

First Collier Books Edition 1991

10 9 8 7

Printed in the United States of America

Contents

■■■■■■■■■■■■■■■■■■■■■■■■■■■■■■■

Acknowledgments

■■■■■■■■■■■■■■■■■■■■■■■■■■■■■■■■

We want to thank all the designers, contractors, craftspeople, and tradespeople who shared their many years of experience with us. With their help, enthusiasm, and contributions we were able to make this book a reality.

Introduction

■■■■■■■■■■■■■■■■■■■■■■■■■■■■■■

As we write this book, we're living in (and working on) our fourteenth house. Over the years we've learned how to deal with contractors we've hired and worked with to do various parts of our remodeling projects. This book is the result of all our experiences, a practical manual for the person about to venture forth into the strange world of home remodeling and building.

How to Be Your Own Contractor is a source book you can refer to again and again for practical, usable information about how to work with contractors, tradespeople, craftspeople, and designers. It answers the two most important questions a homeowner contracting out remodeling work can have. How do I know these people are doing the job right? And what do I do if they aren't?

For the most part we've had positive experiences working with all sorts of contractors. But that's not to say we haven't had to learn the hard way. In one of the first houses we worked on we found an old bathtub that badly needed refinishing. A leaking faucet had gone unchecked for years, leaving the porcelain finish around the drain worn away and rusted.

We called two bathtub refinishers for estimates and were surprised at their bids—both $250. While we were still in shock, out of nowhere came a telephone call from a young man who said he worked for one of the contractors and he'd refinish our tub as a side job for half of what his boss would charge. He said he had all the equipment and experience necessary because he worked full-time refinishing tubs.

That sounded like a good deal to us, so one Saturday morning he showed up, went to work, and, within a few hours, "refinished" the bathtub and collected his $125. As far as we were concerned it looked as good as new. By Tuesday morning, however, the entire area around the drain had bubbled up, and it looked awful.

We, of course, got what we deserved. It was a classic case of how *not* to deal with a contractor. In the first place we didn't ask for references. We made no effort to find out if the man was qualified. We were perfect pigeons looking for a deal, and he saw an easy way to make a fast buck on a side job that he knew he'd never have to stand behind. The only way to find him was a telephone number that turned out to be his mother's. When we called she as much as said, "Look, what did you expect? You get what you pay for." We had paid him in full, so we had no recourse but to admit our mistake. We proceeded to hire one of the original contractors so we ended up spending $375 for a job that should have cost us $250.

In the first section of this book you'll find our guidelines for remodeling and building. We talk a lot about hiring contractors: How do you find a good one? How do you get a contractor to answer your calls? What should be included in a good contract with a contractor? What should you look out for? Are you liable for all the workers who descend on your property?

What about being your own contractor? Is that a good idea?

For do-it-yourselfers, we suggest ways you can work with a professional without impeding the progress of the job. For the majority of you, who want to hire a contractor and leave the work entirely to him or her, we suggest ways to manage the project so it runs smoothly. Whatever your goal, we hope you'll find bits and pieces of information that will make your remodeling or building project less of a hassle.

The second section of the book is devoted to specific contractors and what to expect from them. For example, we tell you what a mason does, then answer such questions as: How much does he charge? Can you save money by working with him? Or, with an exterminator, does he guarantee his work? Do you pay a paperhanger by the hour or by the number of rolls of paper he hangs? We walk you through the general process of each trade and what each contractor does so you have an overview of what to expect. This will help you become a more savvy consumer, someone who can ask key questions of the people you hire.

We begin with design professionals, then get down and dirty with the contractors who deal with the mechanical systems of a house. The two longest sections cover all the contractors who deal with the interior and exterior of your house. Then we move outdoors to the yard and the contractors whom you hire to move the earth around. Lastly, we discuss specialty service and maintenance contractors, such as bathtub refinishers, asphalt sealers, and chimney sweeps.

1

Guidelines for Remodeling and Building

■■■■■■■■■■■■■■■■■■■■■■■■■■■■■■■

Each phase of a remodeling or building project is in itself interesting, challenging, and rewarding. At the beginning your creative juices stir as you compile your dream kitchen "wish list." After sweeping up the remains of a demolished wall you feel a sense of deep satisfaction because you've accomplished your goal. And there's a feeling of finality as you tighten down the paint can lid after the last stroke of your roller completes the fourth wall.

FOCUSING ON THE "BIG PICTURE"

While each individual task has its own reward, these small triumphs can be overshadowed when you have a string of jobs to complete. One of the most frustrating aspects of home construction and remodeling is that overall progress depends on the sequential completion of even the most trivial task. If the materials aren't at the jobsite when the workers are, no work can be done. If the new range hood is delivered without the mounting hardware, the job can't be completed. Plumbing fixtures that arrive damaged or in the wrong color must be reordered. Even on a modest job like replacing a kitchen floor, organization and coordination skills are almost as important as the talent of the worker laying the floor. If your contractor doesn't have conscientious workers and punctual subcontractors, or doesn't have a strong sense of timing and scheduling, even a straightforward project will quickly come to a halt.

Probably the most important lessons we've learned (and are still learning) in all our remodeling is that before you worry about dealing with contractors, you have to decide exactly what you want to do to your house. And that's not easy.

What Do You Really Want?

Before we can tell you how to choose a contractor or determine which design professional will serve you best, you have to know what you want him or her to do for you. You cannot expect a contractor to read your mind. If you tell him "I'm thinking about building a two-story addition that's attached to the kitchen, but maybe to the side bedroom, I'm not sure, and I want it to sort of look like this, but not exactly . . . ," you shouldn't be surprised when he says he's not interested in the job.

Knowing exactly what you want is difficult, probably impossible, before you actually talk to a professional, but you should spend some time fine-tuning your priorities. A good way to do this is to peruse home-related magazines and books, but don't limit your research to them. We found a perfect example of a bookcase we want to build in our living room in the background of a photo in a Spiegel catalog. A friend of ours saw a charming picket fence on Nantucket, snapped a picture of it, and copied the design for his house in the Midwest. When you see something you like, make a quick sketch or get it on film or videotape. Clip pictures of rooms from as many sources as possible and earmark pictures in decorating books. We use a pocket folder to hold the pictures. If you can't bear to tear up magazines, keep a running index of ideas that you like, noting the magazine issue and page number, or photocopy the page.

We have another folder, labeled "Neat Stuff," where we collect pictures of things we'd like to incorporate into future projects. The ideas you save might include a corner detail on a laminated kitchen countertop, a pattern for laying bricks in a patio, or a new product you'd like to consider. If you like it, record the idea, even if you have another use for it in mind. A style of molding that's shown in a picture of a dining room might be exactly right for your bedroom.

If you're an organizer, you might like to have a more detailed filing system, but don't get too carried away or you won't keep it up. By accumulating these ideas, you focus on the look you like. As you change your mind, toss out pictures and replace them with new ones.

You might already have some good design ideas gleaned from homes you've visited. If you've lived in more than one house, remember how your family's lifestyle fit in each one. Your kids can be a great help at this because they seem to remember obscure little tidbits you've long forgotten. Try to recall details, like handy storage places or convenient floor plans. Remember, if you can't be specific about what you want in your new space, it's unrealistic to expect a contractor who doesn't know you and your lifestyle to be able to build it for you.

Seek Design Help

Design professionals, like architects, space planners, interior designers, and landscape architects, play an important role in remodeling and building because they act as interpreters. These professionals are trained or have learned how to listen to your sometimes vague ideas, wants, and dreams, and translate them into living space. There's also a growing number of creative contractors who not only are skilled in the building trades but also have varying backgrounds in design. These general contractors or tradespeople may lack formal design training but have a well-developed eye for solving problems, especially when they're called on to do variations of the same theme.

For example, a contractor whose primary job is remodeling kitchens in old houses has dealt with many homeowners wanting a large eat-in kitchen where there had been a very small one. He or she will work out floor plans that open up pantries and extend kitchen space into an adjoining bedroom or back porch. The remodeler has the experience to take advantage of every bit of space, no matter how small, and will find room to build in bookcases for the gourmet cook or a mud room entrance for a busy household. In some cases these elements become a contractor's trademark. We knew a contractor in Chicago who artfully carved out space for a washer and dryer that backed up to the kitchens in many homes. Another contractor was adept at using sheets of Corian for everything from windowsills to tub enclosures (and, of course, for countertops, too).

Today, more than ever before, good functional design is important. The highest-quality materials and craft are wasted if the end product does not function. It costs no more to remodel a kitchen with an efficient layout than it does to create one with several bottlenecks. Two good-sized bedrooms with a connecting hall and bath add more value to your attic conversion than three tandem bedrooms. Tandem rooms (you have to walk through one to get to the other) might have been tolerated by the last generation of homeowners, but today few see much value in room space for the sake of room space. Unless you have a good handle on exactly what you want, it's well worth the expense to consult with a design professional.

Finding the Right Designer

Finding the right designer is like making a friend. You can talk to many talented people with great ideas, but if you are not on the same wavelength, the relationship won't work. There has to be mutual respect between you and the designer. First impressions are usually lasting when it comes to personal interaction, and you will be doing a lot of interacting before your ideas get to a final plan. Realistically, any designer can help you buy a few pieces of furniture to fit your lifestyle and decor, but if you're in for the long haul of redecorating a whole house or designing an addition, you and the designer should be compatible. You certainly won't like every piece or idea that you're shown, but you should feel that you're being listened to.

Interior designers often exhibit their work in designer showcase house tours. These tours are sponsored by charitable organizations and present as many designers as there are rooms in the house. It's a plume in the cap of designers to be asked to "do" a room, so they invest quite a bit of their time and money in the project. Remodeling contractors, kitchen and space planners, and landscape architects also participate in these showcase houses. The cost of your ticket to one of these tour houses is a donation, and it's money well spent if you want to see examples of several designers' work under one roof.

In chapter 2 we provide specific information about how to find each of these design professionals, what they will do for you, and how to work with them.

Invest in Working Plans

Except for simple replacement or facelift remodeling projects, it's worth the money to pay a professional to create working plans or designs. These are useful in taking your plan out of your head and actually determining whether it's feasible. If there are structural changes involved in your new house or remodeling project, you'll need a written or drawn plan to present to the building department in order to get a permit.

In most areas of the country, you can hire an architect, interior designer, kitchen designer, or space planner for about $50 an hour. Most of the time a general contractor will charge extra for a design and plan. Some kitchen contractors or landscaping firms also charge for a design. If you commission professionals to do the initial design work and then hire them to supervise or carry out the work, the design fee is usually reduced.

CONSIDERING CONTRACTORS

We've been to many parties where the hot topic of conversation has nothing to do with sex, religion, or politics. Instead the discussion revolves around building a house or remodeling one. Who is doing what to their house (and how much it costs) . . . who is doing the work . . . which contractors have a year-long waiting list . . . who is the best person to deal with at the local building department . . . etc., etc. If you can tap into this informal network of information, it can be very help-ful in finding reliable contractors and tradespeople.

Since most of a contractor's business is generated by word of mouth, it's a good idea to start talking about your project and asking questions of anyone who will listen. You can seek the advice of realtors and bankers, but we'd put more stake in what you learn at aerobics class and the barber shop. Look at work trucks in your neighborhood, ring doorbells at houses where you see work being done, and talk to homeowners who have a remodeling project under way and are in the trenches, so to speak, at the time.

If your project will involve contractors with special skills or interests, go to an area where that type of tradesperson or contractor regularly works. For example, if your project in-volves historic restoration, go to an old neighborhood under-going transformation. Make the visit during the week, not on a weekend, so the tradespeople will be working, and you can look for vans or pickup trucks parked in front of jobs in progress. If you like what you see going on, jot down names and phone numbers from the trucks or talk to workers on the job. Talk fast, though, and don't be a nuisance.

One fact you might be surprised to learn is that if the contractors are any good, you'll have to wait for them to work your project into their schedule. The best contractors in any field have plenty of work to keep them busy.

Once you have leads to several contracting firms or design professionals and you have a pretty good idea of what you want, you're ready to make initial contact. Most contractors are listed in the Yellow Pages but rarely do they get cold calls from their listing. Most of the contractors we talked with said referrals from satisfied customers make up the bulk of their workload. Make a list of the names and phone numbers of the contractors you call so you can keep a record of when you called, if you left a message, the response you received, or how quickly the contractors responded, even if it was to tell you they're too busy or can't handle the work.

When you call, you will usually get a recorded message on an answering machine, or if it's a big outfit, you'll reach a secretary. If a contractor maintains an office, it's more likely you'll reach him or her, but getting a busy contractor to call back is not always easy. Contractors who work out of their homes have answering machines and usually screen their calls. These people put in long days at the jobsite, working or supervising their crews, so the last place you'll find them is answering the phone in the evening. The exception to that is a rainy day when you might catch them doing paperwork. Most return their calls when it's convenient for them, usually early in the morning or in the evenings during the week or on Sunday afternoons.

Make it easy for contractors to get back to you by being available. If you're not easy to reach, tell them when the best time is to call you. Introduce yourself and explain how you got their name. If you were impressed with the work you saw at a friend's house, tell them. Don't expect to get a call back from any contractor right away or you'll be in for frustration and disappointment.

Don't pester contractors by calling them at home early in the morning or during the dinner hour. They will call you when it's convenient and probably at a time that's good for you as well if you've left that information. It has been our experience that barraging contractors with phone calls does not make them call back any sooner and usually antagonizes them. Good contractors and tradespeople are professionals in demand. They are independent people who have earned their positions by doing superior work.

You will see throughout this book that we refrain from contractor-bashing as much as possible. We've learned that if you approach tradespeople and contractors as professionals, you will be treated professionally. Of course, we have come across the exception to that rule, and you might, too, but your initial contact should be made with mutual respect.

Not much has been said about an intangible we all use in hiring someone. Call it whatever you like, it's sort of a gut feeling you have about a person. You feel comfortable about having this person in your house. You like the way he or she talks to your kids or pets—whatever it is, it's all part of finding the right person to work in your house.

Getting Bids for Remodeling and Building

Basically there are two types of work involved in remodeling and building—jobs calculated by square footage and jobs involving custom work. Jobs like painting, laying sod, or refinishing floors are calculated by the square foot. The skills required are repetitive and specific to that trade. You can get bids for this type of work and pretty much do comparison shopping.

Anytime you're going to change the structure of your house, however, you're into custom design work, even if it's as simple as a bump-out of a kitchen wall to add a bay window. This type of work is more involved than a square-foot job. Here you might have to deal with changing or expanding the electrical and heating systems. The carpentry work cuts into the exterior siding, creating potential problems of matching new siding with existing surfaces. As straightforward as this job seems, it's still unique to your house.

Work that involves structural changes, such as reworking the mechanical systems of a house or building an addition, is considered custom work by contractors. Even seemingly simple repairs to an older house can offer unique challenges. When you're working with old pipes or antiquated electrical wiring, there are always one or two surprises. Contractors can guess what they'll find when they open a wall, but what they actually find when they get into the heating and cooling systems, not to mention plumbing and electrical lines, can wreak havoc with the best designed plans. Your project is a one-of-a-kind job in a one-of-a-kind house because it's had homeowners altering and changing it.

Bidding for remodeling work is tricky business, and the more experience contractors have, the better they get at it. If the remodeling project is straightforward, the contractors know what to expect; it's not difficult to figure the cost of new materials and the labor needed to install them. The hard part is trying to anticipate possible problems and allow for them in the contract price. The low bidder is not always realistic in assessing the job. If the contractors are too conservative and jack up the price to cover all possible problems, then the estimate will be way out of line.

On the other hand, if the contractors don't provide some cushion for the unknown, then halfway through the job you will find them announcing that things are not going as expected, and more money is needed to complete the job. You as the consumer will have a hard time deciding whether the contractors are justified in asking for more money or whether they just underbid the job to get the work. That's why it is important for you to establish a good working relationship with the contractors you hire. Keep the dialogue open; make it clear to the contractors that you want to know how the job is going and tell them you expect to be notified right away if the unexpected happens.

It is not the contractor's fault if you have a bad pipe that needs to be replaced, but you do have a gripe if the pipe was clearly visible or known to be faulty and the contractor neglected to figure in the cost of its replacement in the estimate. In these circumstances it pays to have a clear contract. Unless what will be done is clearly stated, you and your contractor might expend a lot of energy negotiating after the negotiating is supposedly done.

If contractors were perfectly frank, they would tell you that they really don't know how long it will take them to complete a custom-work job. Of course they won't tell you that. We all make schedules, and so do contractors. They line up work into the future and are always working toward their next job. There are 1,001 things that can happen to upset a schedule and at least 500 usually do. Remember this when a contractor working on a major remodeling job tells you, "I'll start next week and be finished in two weeks." He hopes he will, and maybe even thinks he will, but the truth is, he usually won't. He's giving you the best guess at when he thinks he'll complete the job, but that's what it is—a guess.

It's different if the work is a straightforward job such as painting the bedrooms or laying a new floor because the work is not dependent on other work being completed. For this type of work contractors are likely to know (and tell you) how long they'll take to complete a job.

Our Experience with the "Three-Bid Theory"

When asked about how to get bids for a project, everyone who is supposedly in the know says: Get at least three bids for the job, compare the estimates, and then hire the contractor whose bid came in the middle. Good advice? Maybe—but it's not always possible, or even practical.

If yours is a job like patching a small section of wallboard or plaster or painting a single room, you'll be lucky to find two, let alone three, contractors to bid on the job. Depending on the construction business cycle in your area, you may have five contractors bid on the job or find they're all busy for the next six months and don't need to take on such a small project.

Getting multiple bids or estimates is usually possible and has worked well for us on straightforward installation projects like roofing, flooring, insulation, or drywall—basically anything that is figured by the square foot. Often you can get the bid over the telephone because what you need to know is their going rate for the job.

On major custom-work projects you should try to get more than one bid, but cost alone should not be the deciding factor. Let's use a bathroom makeover as an example. The job is fairly straightforward, replacing old fixtures with three new ones (bathtub, vanity, and toilet). It can involve a general contractor and several subcontractors, e.g., plumbers, electricians, carpenters, drywall hangers, and painters.

Contractor number one comes in and gives you a bid for $5,000, contractor number two's bid is $7,000, and contractor number three's bid is $6,500. The materials are all the same or comparable in quality. However, experience has showed us that the dollar-and-cents figures are not the only thing you have to consider.

There are intangibles as well, like the quality of the contractor's work and experience. Maybe the $5,000 bid came from a contractor whose schedule is open for a few months before he starts a big job. Maybe the strong suit of his crew is framing new houses and he bid your job low to pick up a small job to tide him over. If that's the case, you'll be hiring someone who is a whiz at rough carpentry but not familiar with small bathroom jobs. You run the risk of his workers creating problems that didn't exist, for example, cutting into a plumbing line that's in the floor, or botching the drywall seams because they've rarely hung drywall. It's not likely that he'll be back to fix a mistake when you call him four months later.

The $7,000 came from a contractor who has done bathroom remakes up and down your block and just raised his labor rates to take advantage of a neighborhood ripe for new bathrooms.

The middle bid came from an enthusiastic young guy who's just getting into the business and works for a lower rate because he's on his own and doesn't have other helpers he has to keep busy. But can he handle the job?

In this case, if you consider only the cost and ignore the expertise of these contractors you might be disappointed with your bathroom. The main lesson we have learned in looking over many bids is that all they can tell you is what the job will probably cost. The bid alone cannot tell you if the contractor can bring the job in on time, within budget, and to your satisfaction.

When we first started remodeling, the biggest problem we had was comparing estimates, even for square-foot work. We would get bids on a straightforward job, but when we placed them side by side it was hard to tell which was better.

For example, we were replacing a kitchen floor. We had a brand-name floor and pattern that we picked out and the first floor man we talked with gave us an estimate on the flooring and installation. The second contractor showed us samples of another floor that we thought we liked better, so he gave us an estimate for that floor. The third floor contractor presented his case and said we needed to install underlayment, which was needed under the seamless floor he suggested. His estimate included laying a subfloor under the new floor.

We got these bids over a period of several weeks. When we

sat down to study them, we found they were for three entirely different jobs. We were comparing apples with oranges. We eventually went with our first choice of flooring and gave the job to the first contractor. After doing the same thing on several different projects, we realized that the other contractors lost out because we changed our minds about what we wanted, not because they were unqualified or had priced themselves out of the competition.

Now we stay open to all suggestions from contractors we talk to and ask questions to find out as much as we can about the details of the project. So should you. The more you learn from contractors, the more insight you will gain. You can then make a better decision about which contractor has the best approach, products, design, etc. You should also make yourself as familiar as possible with the products you plan to use.

Choose the estimate of the contractor you think has the best approach and use it as a basis for comparison. Then ask the other contractors to resubmit an estimate based on the specifications in that bid. Some will resubmit; some will refuse—but in the end you can compare the estimates because they will be for similar materials and quality of work.

We've had good luck with contractors who have been in business for at least three years. It's not an easy business to succeed in, so if contractors can hang in there for that long, they're probably going to stay in business. As business people, contractors know their reputation is their best advertisement. If they work in a specific area, like the North Shore of Chicago or the east side of Cleveland, they know that homeowners have a grapevine network to communicate good and bad reports. Longevity in the construction business is an accomplishment in itself. It doesn't guarantee good work, but it's an indication that the business has at least maintained itself. If they're good, reasonable, and dependable, they'll last!

Another consideration is the availability of the contractor. It might be worth the extra money to choose the high-bidding contractor or risk working with a start-up company if they are available *now* and you want to get the project under way. However, we have also accepted a contractor whose bid was high and waited for him because we wanted him and only him to do the job. Cost, reputation, and availability are factors that you have to weigh carefully when evaluating a bid.

The Time and Materials Bid

Some jobs, especially small ones, lend themselves to a working agreement where straight time and the cost of materials are billed. The contractor or tradesperson agrees to do "work for hire" based on an hourly wage plus the cost of the materials used in the project. This is a popular arrangement with individual tradespeople who do side jobs after hours. You can supply the materials or have the contractor purchase them.

An advantage to this arrangement is that the tradesperson does not pad the bill, expecting to find a snag along the way. You pay for only the work completed. The downside of this agreement is that there is no cap on the cost, and no way for the homeowner to know exactly how much a job will total. The tradesperson can say, "It shouldn't take more than five hours." But what if it does?

We try to set a break point so the contractor or tradesperson must inform us when a certain dollar amount of work is accomplished. You can say "Let me know if it's going to run over $150," which helps you keep the lid on the expense.

One point should be made clear in this arrangement. Ask how the tradesperson figures work time. Does it include travel time to and from the job, or is that extra? Do you pay for the worker to collect the building materials? What about driving discarded materials to the local dump? Make sure that the tradesperson keeps track of work time and presents you with an overall itemized statement on the day of reckoning. You should keep track of the worker's hours as well, if that's possible.

The Nuisance Bid

One of the reasons there is such a wide variation in estimates presented for the same work is what's called a nuisance bid. No one likes to be considered a pest or nuisance, but that's exactly what you are to a contractor who is booked solid and doesn't really want to do your job right now. Good contractors will tell you up front they're booked up, but some will bid on the work as insurance against a cancellation in their scheduled workload, so be prepared for a whopper of an estimate.

If you read between the lines of a preposterously high bid, this is what it says: "I am very busy now, but I will work overtime if you pay me enough." The profit each contractor figures into the job is usually in direct proportion to how badly he or she wants or needs the work. At times contractors will bid jobs low just to keep their crews working.

BUILDING PERMITS, LICENSING, BONDING, AND INSURANCE

Because they do not involve alterations to the structure of a house, cosmetic changes like painting and landscaping and small improvement projects do not require a building permit. Nor do minor repairs to the plumbing and electrical systems, like repairing leaky faucets or replacing worn electrical receptacles or switches. Most other work that changes or alters the house does require a building permit.

If you fail to get a building permit and get caught, you can be fined, and your job can be stopped until you get the necessary permits. You might have to tear out new drywall or other finished surfaces for inspectors to look at the plumbing and electrical work. If any work does not meet the building codes in your area, you will have to redo it.

Working under a permit is actually for your own protection. A homeowner who does faulty work that violates the building codes in any way can be held responsible for any mishap that might result from it. Your insurance company might not pay a fire claim, for example, if it is caused by faulty wiring done without the proper permits. You can be sued by subsequent owners of the property for damages for your faulty work.

Aside from the actual cost of the permit and possible increases in your property taxes, we see little reason to avoid getting a building permit. If you don't know anything about how proper footings should be put in or how plumbing fixtures must be vented, then the local building inspector is really working for you. Some contractors, however, don't like building inspectors because they slow down the job.

We have worked with building inspectors and, we admit, sometimes around them. We think you're better off getting the permits or having the contractors get the necessary permits than playing cat and mouse with the inspectors. Go to your building department and find out what permits, if any, are needed. Also find out if the contractors in your area are required to be licensed or bonded.

If the code requires a license, then that should be a criterion for selecting a contractor. In this case, without a license, a contractor can't get building permits. And some work, especially sewer and water-main work, requires that the contractor be bonded or post a bond with the department. The bond is returned after the completion of the work and inspection. Towns and cities don't like unqualified plumbers cutting into or working on public utilities. The bond is also insurance that you will get a decent job done, since the contractor stands to lose a lot of money if the job is not completed to the satisfaction of the building inspector.

You should not do business with a contractor who is not insured. State and local requirements vary, but a contractor should at least carry a worker's compensation and a general liability policy. Licensed contractors with bonding and insurance will gladly show you proof of their policies. It is evidence that they are in business for the long haul, make enough money to pay for insurance, and are smart enough to purchase it.

If you decide to hire a tradesperson without liability insurance to work off hours on a time and materials bid, check with your insurance agent first. Your homeowner's policy might cover such a situation, or you might be able to purchase an extended liability policy. If it doesn't or you can't, hiring an insured contractor or tradesperson is the safer choice—you don't want to expose yourself to unnecessary risk. Assume nothing, and ask every tradesperson to show you a receipt indicating he's a paid-up policyholder.

BEING YOUR OWN GENERAL CONTRACTOR

The profit from job to job will vary, but a general contractor usually tries to keep at least 20 percent of the total cost of each job. This is a hefty chunk of money, so it is tempting for many homeowners to become their own general contractors.

It's been our experience that it's a rare homeowner who makes a good general contractor. To do the job right, you should be at the jobsite every day, have experience working with tradespeople, be very organized and keep good records, and, above all, know something about construction. Because a woman is home all day with the kids doesn't make her a likely candidate. Just because a man worked construction in college doesn't make him good at it either.

Even though you may not see the general contractor at the job every day, the money you pay him or her is well earned. The general contractor is the "mover and shaker" of a project. He or she hires and coordinates the subcontractors, orders materials, and sees they're delivered. If a problem or snag occurs, the general contractor is there to make decisions and keep the work progressing.

One of the greatest obstacles a homeowner–general contractor faces is trying to schedule the job. Planning and preparation take a lot of time. Most phases of construction are interdependent, making it imperative to come up with a clearly defined and realistic work schedule. From beginning to end it's a juggling act to get each tradesperson out so others can begin.

A general contractor hires and rehires a regular group of reliable professional subcontractors throughout the year who are loyal to him. They are more likely to show up on schedule for a steady customer than for your one-time job. A homeowner–general contractor has a tough job competing with a professional general contractor in getting the best subcontractors and keeping them on schedule and in line.

This is not an insurmountable task, but be aware that you will earn your savings. If you have strong organizational skills, manage people on a regular basis, possess a good sense of humor, and do your homework, you might be able to manage your own construction project successfully.

WORKING WITH A CONTRACTOR
AS A DO-IT-YOURSELF HOMEOWNER

When renovating houses we pretty much split the work fifty-fifty between doing it ourselves and hiring contractors. We were able to work along with some of the contractors we hired, but most of the time we worked before the contractors arrived on the job and after they left.

We learned to break down most jobs into two categories: skilled work and the unskilled labor we call grunt work. We concentrated on completing the unskilled jobs, like preparing surfaces, demolishing walls, or removing wallpaper or old carpeting. Tasks like tearing up an old floor or carrying out trash and cleaning up the jobsite are things anyone can do, and you'll save the hours clocked by a laborer and enjoy being part of the work effort if you do them yourself. Also, if you're adept at certain phases of a job, like painting walls, you can take responsibility for them and eliminate them from the contractor's bid.

The reason contractors and tradespeople are reluctant to work side-by-side with you is that you'll most likely slow them down and drive them crazy with questions. Of course there are exceptions. We know plumbers and electricians who don't mind answering our game of twenty questions when we pay them by the hour.

Whatever work you decide you can do, the most important thing to remember is that you must work out exactly what you will be responsible for and what the contractor will do. You should also know how much your labor will reduce the overall cost. Do not sign an agreement, then decide to do some of the work yourself and ask the contractor to knock off money from the estimate.

Being reliable and performing a job to meet the standards of the contractor are important parts of working with him. You have to complete your part of the work when you say you will. If your work isn't ready when it's supposed to be or the contractor's crew has to come in and redo what you've done, you've wasted your time and the contractor's.

GETTING IT IN WRITING: THE CONTRACT

The agreement between you and the contractor or tradesperson you hire can be as simple as a handshake or as formal as a fifty-page single-spaced document. Either agreement can work and neither is any better than the parties agreeing to it. We have found communication is the most important ingredient of any deal.

A written agreement or contract is the best foundation for effective communication. The more detailed the contract, the less room there is for a misunderstanding. Even with a very exact written agreement, you might have to work out some unforeseen details as the job progresses, but having something in writing to start is beneficial for all parties involved.

There are many forms a contract can take. Most large contractors have stock contracts that cover the basics. Below are some of the main points we like to include in contracts we sign. A lawyer might feel differently about our choices, but if the agreement gets too nitty-gritty, some contractors will back off and refuse to do the job. Some of these points you might not be able to get confirmation on; starting and completion dates are often stumbling blocks.

Another factor you should consider is the value of the contract. If you are having a sink replaced for $300 you don't require documents of the same detail as for a $125,000 addition to your house. Have your lawyer look over the contract for a big-ticket job, but a handshake will probably get you through more moderately priced improvements.

An agreement or contract between you and an architect, design professional, or contractor should clearly spell out who is involved in the contract and the work that will be done. It should include the contractor's name, business address, phone number, and license number (when a license is required). It should state the name and address of the homeowner and, if it's different from the homeowner's address, the location of the work to be completed.

Here are some points to look for in a basic contract in layperson's words, since we are not lawyers.

Job Description

The nature of the work to be done should be carefully detailed. The exact area where the work will be performed, with dimensions and a working plan, should be part of the document. The nature of the demolition, trash removal, renovation, reconstruction, and finishing work should all be specified. If you have any questions about who does what, work them out with the contractor and get the answers in the contract.

Materials Specifications

All materials should be listed by brand name, type, model, number, color, and size. The make and model number of all appliances should be included. Avoid ambiguous descriptions like "siding to match existing." Pick out a particular siding that matches and specify it exactly. Your idea of a match can be far from what the contractor thinks is acceptable.

Starting and Completion Dates

Some contractors will balk at this clause. Even if you agree on firm dates there are many uncontrollable circumstances that might alter them. Some contractors will agree to just about anything to get the job but have no intention of showing up on the starting date.

You can try to include a penalty clause stating what will happen if the contractor misses these dates but the contractor, in turn, might insist on an early completion clause where you pay a bonus if the job is finished early.

One clause that a good contract should have but some contractors refuse to sign is a clause allowing you to use the balance of the money owed the contractor to hire someone else to complete the job if the contractor does not work on the job or neglects to complete it during a stipulated time period.

Another incentive for the contractor to start your job on time is for you to keep the advance money as small as possible and withhold it until the job actually starts. Once the contractor gets your money you have very little leverage. The same is true for the final payment; always try to keep the value of the work completed by the contractor higher than the money you have paid out.

Building Permit

Find out if a building permit is required for the work you are contracting for. If it is, insist that one be taken out in the name of the contractor, not in your name. This makes the contractor, not you, responsible if any work is not acceptable to the inspector. Otherwise, you might be financially responsible for correcting the work so it meets the building code. Also have the contractor responsible for posting all bonds.

Cleanup and Debris Removal

Most municipal garbage trucks will not pick up large amounts of construction debris. To rent a Dumpster and have it delivered to a jobsite is expensive, so it's important to spell out who will be responsible for the removal of debris and building materials. Also, agree where the Dumpster will be deposited on your property before it is delivered.

Leaving the jobsite in "broom clean" condition every day is an important stipulation if the jobsite is part of your home and your family has to live there after the workers leave each day. Clarify who does the cleanup and where the daily refuse from the job goes.

Workers' Behavior

If you don't want workers using your bathroom, make a provision for a portable toilet in the contract. Specify in the contract who will pay for the toilet and who will be responsible for ordering one delivered to the jobsite. And if you're worried about noise, a contract can specify "no loud music allowed."

Change Order Clause

Make all changes to the original specifications in writing. "While you're at it, why don't we do the . . ." or, "as long as you're here, let's change the . . ." is often the way such changes are initiated. If it's expressed in light conversation between you and the contractor, it's easy to forget that these modifications are not included in the bid for the work and will likely cost you more money. To avoid being stunned at the reckoning for payment, sign and receive a copy of any and all changes. A change order is a written document that spells out any changes or additions to the job that are outside of what's specified in the contract. Some contractors may want additional funds up front to pay for materials and services that are not covered in the contract.

Pay Periods

A schedule of payments should be spelled out. There are various ways this can be done, but insist that the payments do not get ahead of the work actually completed.

Some contracts require payment in thirds. For example, for a $10,000 kitchen remodeling job you would pay $3,500 when signing the contract, another $3,500 midway through the project, and the remaining $3,000 upon completion of the job.

You can also set up what is known as a draw schedule, which details how and when payments will be made for work completed. This works well on larger projects with many phases. One way is to divide the total amount into fifths, paying out 20 percent when you sign the contract, 20 percent when the foundation work is done, 20 percent when the exterior work is completed, 20 percent when the systems (plumbing, electrical, and heating) are operating, and the final 20 percent when the interior finishing work is completed.

To help keep the work schedule moving along, keep a "punch list" of work left to be completed by a contractor before you pay the monies due.

Arbitration

The best way to avoid a legal dispute between you and the contractor is to stipulate how differences will be decided. Decide on a method of arbitration you will both submit to before going to the legal system and include it in the contract. Often the local Better Business Bureau will act as an arbitrator in disputes between homeowners and contractors.

If arbitration will not settle the dispute, you can seek a settlement in your local small claims court where you can represent yourself. Most of these courts limit the amount of the suit to a maximum of $2,000. Disputes over larger amounts must be taken to the regular court system and usually require the services of a lawyer.

Do-It-Yourself Work

If you plan to do some of the work yourself, put that plan in writing. Spell out the exact job description of what you will do and when you will complete the work.

Mechanic's Lien

What happens if the general contractor is dishonest and uses your money for purposes other than work on your house? In a major remodeling project or new house construction, the general contractor hires subcontractors to do discrete phases of the project. You assume the subs and materials suppliers are being paid by the general contractor (presumably with the money from your payment) but learn they haven't been paid. Any or all of them can put a lien against your home. To prevent this from happening, add a "release of lien" clause, also called a "waiver to the contract," which should free you of this responsibility.

BEING THERE

Even if you have hired a good general contractor to supervise a project, you as the homeowner need to be there and manage what's happening (or not happening) to keep the job on track. Just being there gives you a tremendous edge throughout the duration of the project. Ask everyone who has had a home built long-distance and they will all say they regret not being able to see firsthand what was being done. Building plans are misinterpreted, walls get put up where they're not supposed to be, closets are framed in at the wrong end of a bedroom—any number of mistakes can happen if there's not a lot of attention paid to detail.

The same is true for a small remodeling job in the house you live in. If no one is home during the day when the work is being performed, make it a point every evening when you return to check out what's happened that day. It's not a bad idea to keep a homeowner's log to record what work was completed and note if there are any mistakes or corrections to be made.

If you're there during the day, you can catch the small details that need watching or be there to talk to the tradespeople when they have questions. What comes up are not usually major decisions, but things like where you want the towel bars to be placed in the bathroom or how you want the light switches to be wired. If you're not there you might come home to find the electrician has wired the switches so that in a gang of three the first switch controls the fan, the second one the tub light, and the third the overhead light for the room. Wouldn't it have made more sense to have had the first switch control the overhead light? Of course, but you can't assume everyone would agree.

TIMING IS EVERYTHING: IMPROVEMENTS IN A BUSY HOUSEHOLD

What appears to be a simple project can often take much longer than anticipated. Never, never build in disaster by scheduling the completion of a project too close to a special event, like your annual Christmas party or your child's graduation. How many times have we been guilty of painting the bathroom hours before guests arrive? You put unnecessary pressure on yourself, your family, and your workers.

Use an event as an incentive to complete a job, make it the proverbial "carrot," but not without providing yourself that cushion of time we call the fudge factor. Half of the home improvements we've made would probably still be unfinished if we hadn't established a deadline. Our scheduling rule is simple: estimate how long it will take and then triple it. This holds true whether you hire someone to do the work or do it yourself.

Here's a real-time timeline: you can easily spend a month or two finding a contractor for a basic job like finishing the walls, ceilings, and floor in a basement. If you're lucky, your work can get scheduled within six months. Let's be realistic and say eight months from the first time you talk to the contractor. Figure a month or two with the workers there and it's been almost a year from the time you began planning the project.

When you're considering an improvement, make sure everyone in the family knows about it—how long it could take and how the work will affect their daily lives. Let's take a straightforward job like replacing the kitchen floor. The project seems simple enough: choose a new resilient flooring material sold by a reputable local flooring contractor, give them money, schedule the installation, and wait for it to happen.

A glitch can occur anywhere along the way. The carpenter sent out to remove the old flooring discovers you have three too many layers of flooring underneath the existing one. All layers must be removed, which compounds labor costs and eats up time. The material comes in, but it's damaged and must be returned and reordered. The old flooring layers are removed, the new material arrives, and the installer has a death in the family and can't make it. Murphy's Law applies when remodeling: if something can go wrong, it will. There's no limit to what can delay what seems like a perfectly simple little home-improvement project.

How this affects the people who use that kitchen daily varies. At some point movable appliances like the refrigerator and stove, the table, and other furnishings are relocated. The first few days of feeding a household with the refrigerator on the back porch brings out the old pioneer spirit in all of us. After that, however, the challenge and inconvenience of camping out in our own house deteriorates. You spend a lot of time and money eating out on a regular basis.

If we seem to dwell on the timing aspect of a remodeling project, it's because missed deadlines are the greatest grievance homeowners have against contractors. To survive a remodeling project you have to be flexible and that's not easy with the demands of family and working life. The solution is simple: don't box yourself into a tight schedule by beginning a project with a rigid completion date. Wait until your family's schedule is relaxed, and you'll have time to watch and enjoy the progress.

When the dust has settled and the contractors are long gone, you'll experience a classic case of "selective memory." You'll be surprised how quickly you forget the hassles and inconveniences you endured and see only how the work has created a better home for you and your family.

2

Design Professionals

■■■■■■■■■■■■■■■■■■■■■■■■■■■

Is spending money on the design of a new house or remodeling project a good idea? Yes, most definitely. One of the reasons many people are reluctant to call in an architect or professional trained in design is because they think all they will get for their money are some nice drawings. There's nothing tangible—no floors to stand on, walls to touch, or hardwood cabinets to open and close.

But that's the essence of a good design: you don't see it. A well-designed floor plan, for example, should flow naturally and encompass the lifestyles of the people who use it. Some homeowners are intimated by professionals like interior designers. They fear they will come in and fussy up their home, making it look more like a display than real living space.

The fact is professional designers can save homeowners money. For example, a landscape architect can come up with a long-range plan for your yard. Instead of purchasing a hodgepodge of plantings, you can wait for specials and sales to purchase trees and shrubs that will become integral parts of a beautifully landscaped yard.

Who knows better than a space designer how to eke out every inch of usable space in a small closet? Sure, you can find storage solutions in your house, but you are not thinking storage all day long. The solution that was hammered out for another client might be the answer to your problems, too.

In this section we'll consider the ins and outs of hiring design professionals. In many cases you can get their services free or at reduced rates with the purchase of materials.

ARCHITECTS

Drive down any street and chances are you can spot a house with an addition. Other houses on that same street might have additions but they are hard to distinguish. It would be foolhardy to say that the second group of houses all had additions designed by architects, but it would be safe to say that if each group of homeowners spent the same amount of money on their additions, the second group got a better deal.

The square-foot cost of construction is so high today that just building haphazard additional space seldom pays off. The addition or remodeling project must add to the function of the house for you to receive full value from your renovation or construction investment. The design element of any project is important and should not be overlooked. Consider seeking the advice of an architect or another design professional for even a modest project.

Architects are professionals who hold degrees in architecture and other related areas and are licensed by the state. Most architects are also certified by the American Institute of Architects (AIA). The most basic task an architect performs is to transform your ideas into a buildable structure. Architects are familiar with all phases of construction and know the local building and zoning codes.

One step below a licensed architect is a designer. These professionals can hold degrees in architecture or design but are not licensed by the state and therefore cannot call themselves architects. A kitchen planner is an example of this type of design professional. Designers can be highly trained but they aren't permitted to design the structural part of a building by law. All commercial and most residential structures must be designed by licensed architects or bear the stamp of a licensed structural engineer.

For example, a kitchen planner can plan everything inside your new kitchen, but if the roof requires raising or a wall must be moved, the plan must be drawn up by a licensed architect. Or the kitchen planner might draw up the plan but it must be approved and stamped by an architect or structural engineer. In most localities major structural changes must have this approval or you won't be able to get a building permit.

Besides being able to design structures an architect must be able to translate your vague concept into reality. For this reason, you should search for an individual with whom you feel some rapport. If you see a house being built or an addition you like, stop and ask who designed it. Also ask friends and neighbors for recommendations. Compile a referral list or, if you come up empty with personal referrals, contact the local chapter of the AIA for a list of local firms.

Some firms specialize in large commercial structures and do an occasional residence, other firms specialize in residences and small commercial buildings. Choose a firm that has experience in designing the type of structure you want to build.

You will be working closely with your architect so compatibility is a must. You stand to get the most from your relationship with the architect if you are both on the same wavelength. During your first meeting, before you make any commitment, observe the architect's initial reaction to your project. If there is little enthusiasm at the start or you have trouble communicating, move on.

Architects are independent professionals and have flexible methods of compensation. In many cases their fee is 15 percent of the total construction cost. This figure can, of course, vary. For smaller projects an architect will charge an hourly rate, or a fixed fee can sometimes be agreed upon.

Whatever the arrangement you end up working out with the architect, set it down in a formal contract. The AIA provides a standard contract form that many architects use. Make sure your agreement spells out exactly what you and the architect will do. Will the architect be responsible for the design and its implementation? Will he or she take on the supervision of the subcontractors and check on the progress of the workers as the project proceeds? Who is responsible for making changes in the work order, should any be required? Set up a working schedule and make sure that the architect knows when you expect the project to be started and completed. Decide on a budget for the project and spell out exactly how the architect will be compensated and when.

How much you want the architect to do depends on your particular situation. Here is how a major remodeling project might be carried out under the supervision of an architect.

First of all, you and your architect have a preliminary meeting to discuss the project and your budget. Together, you work through the initial concept from pictures or sketches you have compiled. The architect then refines these ideas into a set of rough, but fairly complete, sketches for your consideration, and you go over them during a second meeting. At this point all of the major components of your project should be worked out to your satisfaction and within your budget.

From the rough drawings, the architect has a set of working plans drawn up that are complete and detailed. These drawings, along with the specifications and a stock list of materials, are necessary for you to get accurate bids from contractors. The architect can recommend contractors that he or she has worked with before, or you can send the plans out to contractors of your own choice for bidding the job. This can take a couple of months. You and the architect then review the bids and make some modifications if they are way out of line with the original budget. This process involves the "C" word, *compromise*, because few concepts can actually be translated into reality within the original budget.

You award the contract to a builder or employ the architect to oversee the construction. If the architect is not involved in the construction he or she should make periodic inspections of the construction site to check on the progress of the job.

INTERIOR DESIGNERS AND DECORATORS

An interior designer not only provides professional design help but also sells most everything that is used in the decoration of your house. An interior designer meets with clients to discuss their decorating needs and then makes suggestions about how to translate these ideas into a workable arrangement of furniture, wall coverings, and accessories.

A professional organization, the American Society of Interior Designers (ASID) specifies that its members have training and certification to prove they know about building codes and structural requirements. An ASID-certified designer has the expertise to deal with an extensive remodeling project and has invaluable contacts with specialty contractors. Interior designers are excellent sources for finding a good general contractor, and specialty contractors as well.

Many interior designers work on their own, while some join with other designers in a consortium to offer their design services. As a business operator, a designer is required to have a license. Designers usually have access to a larger selection of materials and furnishings than the general public. Often they have a specialty. For example, a designer with a background in traditional or Victorian furnishings will specialize in that particular decor. Designers can also bring their customers into large regional trade showrooms located in the larger urban areas. These showrooms offer a wide array of furniture, carpeting, and accessories.

Most interior designers have a broad knowledge of materials such as carpeting and wallcoverings and offer that expertise along with suggestions for furniture arrangements and window treatments.

An interior designer can help with something as simple as choosing wall-to-wall carpeting (actually, that isn't so easy) to a major redecoration project requiring new floor coverings, furnishings, and wall and window treatments for an entire house.

Since many designers are involved with remodeling projects they have a good understanding of construction. They can help you incorporate a lighting plan into a room so that the necessary electrical work is done during the construction, not afterwards, when it's far more costly.

Choosing an interior designer is not like picking out an appliance dealer. You're shopping for much more than a product and a rock-bottom price. You want an interpreter, someone who listens to what you say and translates your ideas into reality. Most designers get new clients who are referrals from satisfied customers. The old gossip line is still a reliable source of who is doing what to whose house. But don't overlook a new designer in town. Often you'll find a new designer can more than make up for a lack of experience with fresh ideas. A new designer is also anxious to establish a base of clients.

You can get leads to interior designers from many sources. When you see a room that appeals to you in your local newspaper's home section, look to see who is credited as the designer. You can window-shop for a designer at local showcase houses.

Like most design professionals, interior designers have a flexible billing arrangement. For large decorating projects most designers work on a cost-plus arrangement in which the designer sells you materials, furnishings, and so on with a commission tacked on. This commission can be anywhere from 15 percent up. Still, on a large project it might actually be less expensive to work with a designer than to furnish the house yourself, since many designers will pass some of their wholesale discount on to you, helping to offset their fee.

On smaller projects most designers charge an hourly fee that can run anywhere from $40 up. How a particular designer charges is an important question to ask at your initial meeting.

Another way to get design advice is to shop at a furniture store that employs a staff of interior designers. Sometimes the design fee is deducted if you spend a specified amount in the store. For example, if you spend $2,500, a $250 design consultation fee might be deducted from your bill.

You get the most for your money when working with a interior designer if you have a clear idea of what you want. Of course, this is not so easy—if you knew exactly what you wanted, you wouldn't need a designer—but doing a little homework before meeting with a designer will help. We found that it helps to collect pictures from books or magazines that show the kind of look you're hoping for in your home.

If you have long-range plans to buy new furnishings and shopping is not your favorite pastime, you'll be well served to work with an interior designer from the very beginning. You then can work together to create a long-term plan and realistic budget so the result is a room (or rooms) designed and furnished to meet your lifestyle and taste.

A word about decorators. For specific services, such as upholstery or a custom window treatment, you can use the free services of a decorator who is also a trained salesperson working through large retailers like J.C. Penney Co. and Sears Roebuck & Co. Many of these decorator services are available for in-home consultations. The Decorating Den is another such service requiring no fee through which you can select fabric, carpeting, wallcoverings, and window treatments.

Just about anyone can call him or herself a decorator; there is no formal training required. (Don't confuse an interior designer with a decorator.) There are, however, many excellent decorators who will give you sound advice and service.

What an interior designer or decorator cannot do for you is make decisions, so don't waste their time (and your money) if you have no idea what you want. What is frustrating for the professional designer is to deal with indecisive clients— homeowners who don't know what they want or how much they can spend. It all goes back to your taking the responsibility of knowing the look you want and your budget and then having the good sense to hire a professional to help you achieve it.

KITCHEN PLANNERS

Do you know that there should be at least forty-eight inches between a sink cabinet and kitchen island so there's space to open and close doors? Obscure information for some, but essential design knowledge for anyone remodeling a kitchen. A kitchen planner knows those specs, along with many other such details. In the hardworking confines of today's kitchen, these are the details that make the difference between one that is just acceptable and a kitchen tailor-made for your family.

A kitchen planner is someone who specializes in designing kitchens and who works independently, is associated with a remodeling or contracting firm, or is an employee of a kitchen showroom/dealer. A certified kitchen designer is a trained professional associated with the National Kitchen and Bath Association. Kitchen planners can advise you on cabinetry, work surfaces, lighting, appliances, and, of course, making the most of your available space.

If you're buying cabinets and appliances from a showroom/ dealer you may find the services of their planner are free or will be rebated to you when you buy a certain amount of materials from them. Kitchen designers and planners who operate as independent contractors require a business license and usually charge an hourly fee ranging from $35 on up.

A kitchen planner can come up with an overall floor plan that will give you the layout for cabinets, appliances, islands, etc., or he or she can take the design concept one step further and draw up the working plans necessary to begin construction. The present trend is for remodeled kitchens to grow in size, encompassing adjoining rooms, and consequently they're often designed with much more than just preparing and serving food in mind.

When you hire a kitchen planner you'll be surprised at the questions you're asked. Do you chop a lot of vegetables and fruit? Do you need a large bin for storing bulky bags of dry dog food? Do the kids do their homework in the kitchen during meal preparation? How many cooks use the kitchen at one time? Do you use a microwave oven for defrosting, reheating leftovers, or food preparation? To get answers to these questions a planner will often make a point to be present at a typical mealtime in your home to see just how you and family members function in the kitchen.

It's wise to spend a lot of analytical time in the kitchen before contacting a planner. This will be a big help in determining what you want in a new kitchen design. An easy way to decide on the features you'd like to include is to finger what you don't like about your existing kitchen. Keep a pad where you can jot down your observations, good and bad: you need storage near the microwave oven for all its dishware . . . you hate where your dishwasher is located . . . you want more counter space near the oven and multiple electric outlets for appliances . . . you want a boiling water dispenser in the sink and a larger sink for washing your large roasting pan.

Since you'll be working closely with a kitchen planner (and revealing your innermost eating habits!), it's important that you relate to him or her honestly. Without your candid responses about how you live, a planner can't create a design that really works for you.

Because of the complexities involved in even a modest kitchen design and the large amount of money usually involved in kitchen renovation, we feel the money spent on the design helps realize the best return for your remodeling dollar.

SPACE PLANNERS

Adding new shelves and storage bins to an overburdened closet can almost double its usable storage space. You'll get the most out of your closet renovation budget if you take the time to talk with a space planner.

Closet specialty shops located across the country sell shelving components and offer storage planning services to their customers. These shops train their sales staff in space management and work with customers in a variety of ways. They'll work with you on an "à la carte" basis, charging you a consulting design fee for working plans. This usually runs around $50. You can install the new shelving and components yourself, or you can have them design the storage and then carry out the installation, in which case they usually drop their design fee. Before you go to one of these shops, make a rough sketch of your closet, with dimensions. Don't forget to indicate which way the closet door opens—this is key to the design.

Independent space planners require a business license to operate and charge an hourly fee from $25 and up. Most of these professionals specialize in more than just closet design and are adept at bringing order to a chaotic home office or a dangerously cluttered garage. They offer design solutions for problems like transforming the catchall bedroom into a nursery (and finding space throughout the house for all the stuff that was in it).

Space planners have the advantage of knowing the ins and outs of installing all different types of storage systems. They have access to various systems and the many optional accessories that can be used to customize a storage unit. Typically you'll have a choice between plastic-coated wire systems and laminated particleboard. Many space planners have an installer to whom they subcontract the actual installation work. They act as supervisors to make certain the job gets done right.

A typical job might involve a space planner creating a design to best organize a new master bedroom walk-in closet. Since you've probably spent a lot of money on the new room, why settle for a shelf and a couple of hooks that the builder installs? The closet planner will ask a lot of questions to determine exactly what you want to store and how the space can work for you and your needs.

After taking thorough measurements of the space, the planner draws up a design and construction plan. You'll review the plan and decide who will make the installation.

LANDSCAPE ARCHITECTS AND DESIGNERS

To some people the idea of paying someone to tell them where to plant a tree is downright ridiculous. Unfortunately, it's those very same people who make expensive mistakes. They begin by buying shrubs and trees without knowing just how large the trees will grow. When the lovely rhododendron they planted next to the foundation grows to full size, they can't see out their living room windows. And when the sprawling pine tree shading their backyard reaches maturity, it's so high it tangles in the power lines it was planted beneath. "Plan ahead" is exactly what a landscape design professional is trained to do, so the investment you make in plantings will be for the long rather than the short term.

You can get design advice for your yard and garden from individual professionals as well as through nurseries, landscaping services, and deck contractors. A landscape architect has been college educated and passed a state certification test, while a landscape designer may not have as much formal education. Both should be licensed. What makes these professionals valuable to homeowners is their experience working in your particular area. They know about the composition of the soil, the weather, growing conditions, and plants and trees that thrive in that environment.

A landscape architect or designer charges clients in much the same way an architect does. When working with one through a nursery or landscaping service, the design fee is often deducted if all the plantings are purchased and planted by the firm.

A typical job for a home involves full drawings of the home and lot with clearly drawn and identified trees, shrubs, garden areas, and walkways. The drawings look like blueprints, with the outline of the house surrounded by circles and shapes denoting the spread of the mature trees and garden beds. For a sloped lot or site you can expect to find drainage and terracing solutions that specify plantings as well as necessary building materials, such as stone or pressure-treated lumber. A cutaway cross section will detail any construction that is suggested.

A landscape architect or designer is often called in to solve a particular problem, but such services can be used by any homeowners who want their outdoor property to become an important extension of their lifestyle. Having an overall plan for the exterior space of our house has worked for us. With a master plan in hand we have added trees, flower beds, etc., in small increments. Such a plan allows you to fill in the missing components over several years, knowing that when completed the yard will be a well-thought-out whole, designed to suit your needs. Without such a plan to work from, you run the risk of creating a hodgepodge of plantings that do little to enhance your yard.

3

Mechanical Systems

■■■■■■■■■■■■■■■■■■■■■■■■■■■■

The intricate maze of pipes, wires, coils, tubes, lines, flues, and ducts that run through the walls, ceilings, and floors of a house go virtually unnoticed until there's a breakdown in one of its systems. That's when you need to call in a contractor with a specialty in the mechanical systems of a house.

Plumbers and electricians are licensed by the state and make up the largest percentage of these contractors. Other specialty contractors you might require are heating and cooling experts, security system engineers, and specialists in fireplaces and woodburning stoves.

When you're involved in building a room addition, these mechanical contractors often work closely together. On new construction, the mechanical systems are installed within the rough framing of a house before the sheets of drywall go up. Any work done at this early stage of construction is more cost-effective than retrofitted or add-on items.

These specialists offer a broad base of experience in their respective fields. An established firm in an old neighborhood might have serviced your house in the past. These contractors are keenly aware of the local competition and aren't shy about discussing their past accomplishments. In recently developed areas the contractors might be newly established or offshoots of older firms. In either case, you're dealing with skilled tradespeople.

If you saw the movie *The Money Pit*, you'll remember the contractors were portrayed in less than a favorable light. Their specialized knowledge gave them a position of power over the unsuspecting fledgling first-time homeowners. To help you avoid mistakes dealing with mechanical contractors, you should know what they do and how to find reputable firms.

In this chapter we offer a few suggestions that should be helpful. In twenty years of working around old houses we've met some very colorful tradespeople. Surprisingly, most, but not all, of these relationships have worked out okay.

There is no magic formula for hiring electricians, for example, but if you know what they do, how they are regulated, and have a few key things to look for, you will be well armed.

PLUMBING CONTRACTORS AND PLUMBERS

The water and drainpipes in your house are usually installed by plumbers who work for a plumbing contractor. Plumbing contractors are licensed by the state and the locality where they work. Municipalities are especially concerned that only qualified licensed contractors work on public sewer and water lines. All local building codes require that only licensed contractors perform plumbing for hire.

There is a distinction between a licensed plumbing contractor and a plumber. All licensed contractors are plumbers, but not all plumbers are licensed. This is an important distinction. A licensed plumbing contractor can have many plumbers working under his or her license. The contractor is responsible for their work and for seeing that the job meets all the building codes. If the plumbers don't follow the code or do inferior work, the contractor will be held financially liable. This is not the case if you hire one of these workers as an individual to do a side job. He or she may be a union plumber but may or may not hold a license.

If you are going to hire a plumber to do any major work, especially work that involves the public sewer or water main, make sure that the plumber or contractor is licensed, insured, and bondable. Most municipalities require that contractors post a bond whenever they work on the public sewer or water main. Make certain that the people you hire are bondable, otherwise you may have to provide a cash bond, which amounts to several thousand dollars for a major project. Then, if their work does not pass inspection by the plumbing inspector, you may lose your bond money.

A plumbing contractor will usually provide a written bid for a job. Small plumbing repairs and remodeling projects can be contracted on an hourly rate plus cost of materials. The average hourly rate for a plumber is $35. The written proposal should specify exactly what will be done, the materials used, and the type, style, or brand names and style numbers of each fixture to be installed.

In order for you to get comparable bids from several contractors they have to be bidding on the same job. Decide on the fixtures and other relevant parts of the project before you put the job out for bids. Don't let one plumber talk you into a one-piece fiberglass tub when what you really want is a cast-iron tub with tile. The tub systems are not the same and don't cost the same. The bid with the fiberglass tub will be lower, because the plumber is bidding on a less expensive job. If you make changes in the specifications, allow all the contractors bidding on the job to make comparable changes in their bids.

Depending on the housing market in your particular area, you might find it surprisingly difficult to get plumbers to come over and look at a small project, let alone give you a bid. When people are buying houses, good contractors can be hard to find. We have found ourselves choosing a plumber not on reputation or price but on availability. This is *not* the way to choose a contractor. But in the real world it is not always possible to get several plumbers, each having a good, sound reputation, to bid on your job and begin work when you want them to.

Ideally it is in your best interest to get everything in writing for even a modest project, but some plumbers won't want to bother with small jobs like repairing leaky faucets or clearing clogged pipes. In that case they'll usually quote you an hourly rate, which might require a minimum of two hours or include travel time.

For a project like remodeling a bathroom or kitchen, most plumbers or plumbing contractors want a deposit before they start the job. A cash advance of between 15 to 20 percent of the estimated final cost to cover start-up costs and some of the materials cost is standard. Remember, though, the only leverage you have with a contractor is your purse strings. Try to keep the value of the work completed more than your total payments at all times until the job is done.

Architects and builders usually have lists of plumbing contractors with whom they have successfully worked in the past. If you are looking for a plumber yourself, make sure the contractor is experienced in the type of work you need done. We have found this especially important for remodeling work. Plumbers whose experience is primarily in new construction don't know the challenges of remodeling. Tucking a powder room in under a stairway takes a fair amount of creative plumbing. Installing new pipes where they were not designed to go without tearing the whole house apart takes experience. The more experience your plumber has with remodeling jobs, the better it is for you. Personal references provide your best leads, but don't overlook the local paper. There is usually a "Services For Sale" section, and most of the local tradespeople advertise there.

If you are working directly with the plumbers, you must schedule the work so that all rough carpentry work is complete. The plumbers can then rough in the drain and supply lines. They will have to cut and drill holes through some of the framing so the pipes can pass. Good plumbers will be careful not to weaken the floor or wall structure by cutting away too much in order to make it easy to install the pipes.

Depending on the demands of your local building codes, the rough drain and supply lines are inspected and sometimes pressure-tested. Then and only then can the drywall be installed to enclose the plumbing.

There is ample opportunity for you to do some of the work necessary to remodel a typical bathroom or kitchen. Much of the actual work plumbers do involves demolition, not installation. Most of them don't like this part of a project and will gladly leave it to you. You can demolish walls and remove the old fixtures, anything that does not directly involve pipes. The trick is to work out just what you can do to help plumbers before and after they leave the job.

Negotiate this working arrangement with the plumbers before they prepare a bid. Arrive at a clear understanding of the work you'll be doing. If the job is remodeling a bathroom and your job is to remove all the old fixtures, make sure you understand how to disconnect the water lines that run to them.

Find out what condition the plumbers expect to find the bathroom in. Do they expect the walls to be stripped down to studs or just the tile removed from them? What about the ceiling and floor? Discuss all the details of the job beforehand so everyone involved knows what's expected. Work out the timing so plumbers don't show up to run new water lines and find you haven't done your share of the job. Make sure you know exactly what work you have to complete before they can start.

You might have to ask several plumbers before you find one who will agree to this type of arrangement. Most plumbers we have worked with were willing to let us do at least the demolition part of the job. Hammer out the working agreement before the job starts and, for goodness' sake, make sure you live up to your end of the bargain.

ELECTRICIANS

The local power (utility) company in your area provides your house with electrical service, but once that power passes through the meter, it's your responsibility. That's where an electrician comes in. Building codes virtually everywhere require that only licensed electricians do electrical work, but many of the codes make an exception that allows homeowners to do electrical work on their own homes, but that work must still be seen by a building inspector. This rule doesn't apply to small repairs and installations (fixing a faulty plug, installing a dimmer switch), which are so simple that no one is expected to get an electrical permit to do the work.

When it comes to a home addition or remodeling project,

the electrical work must meet all national and local codes and pass an inspection. Unless you are acting as your own general contractor, the electrical work is usually hired out to an electrical subcontractor by the general contractor.

To be licensed by the state, electricians must pass a certification test showing they have competency and knowledge in the field. Many local municipalities require that electricians have a local license in addition to the state license. Check with your building department for the required qualifications of electricians in your area.

Electrical contractors should have and be able to show proof of liability insurance. Most areas require an electrician to carry it as well as worker's compensation. If the electrician is not properly insured and bonded, you leave yourself open to potential lawsuits should someone be injured while working at your house. It might not be a bad idea to check with your insurance representative to see what kind of additional protection your homeowner's insurance provides.

Depending on the type of work to be done, some towns require posting a compliance bond. Whenever electrical services are upgraded or installed, electrical contractors are often required to post such a bond to protect the city against damage to its utilities. Compliance bonds are also protection for homeowners since the city will not refund the bond to contractors until all work has passed inspection.

Remember, if the electrical contractor's work does not pass inspection, you won't be able to close up the walls and continue the job. When the electrical contractor is finished with the rough-in wiring, don't allow any other workers to cover the walls until you've had a successful electrical and plumbing inspection.

Most jobs come to a halt if the walls can't be closed up, so reliability should be high on your list when you check the references of electrical contractors. You can go through the ads in the Yellow Pages to find an electrical contractor, but the most reliable source is a personal referral. Since electrical contractors are licensed and all their work must be inspected, you are pretty well assured of getting a good job.

New construction is straightforward with no surprises, so most electrical contractors figure a job on a cost per opening. Receptacles, switches, and lights are all considered openings because they penetrate the wall. A typical opening consists of a box, the wire needed to bring electricity to the box, a wiring device (receptacle, switch, or light), and cover. An additional charge is added for the "home run" or, in layperson's terms, the wires that lead back to your power panel. Heavy-duty wiring for stoves, air conditioners, and furnaces are figured separately, as is the installation of the main electrical panel.

Remodeling jobs, on the other hand, often require fishing wires through existing walls and can take more time. There are also many variables and unexpected problems that can make this type of work expensive. Most contractors use a combination of per-opening cost and an hourly rate of $35 to figure a remodeling job.

For the contractor to be able to give you an accurate estimate, you must know how many outlets, switches, lights, and other electrical installations you need. The building codes have a lot to say about their locations, so make certain your plan meets all code requirements. An electrician who suggests you need more outlets is not trying to con you. Generally, electrical codes require that outlets be placed no farther than six feet from doors and windows and be no more than twelve feet apart. The idea here is to locate outlets so that whatever you want to plug into an outlet will not require a cord longer than six feet.

Whether you're building a new house or remodeling,

changes or add-ons, such as switches, outlets, or lights, are more expensive than if you included them in the original bid. Careful planning will save you money.

Unless you are doing all the electrical work yourself there is not much opportunity for you to participate in this type of work to save money. If you have experience working with electricity you might try to arrange for the electrician to work on only the rough wiring. You can then install the outlets, switches, covers, and other devices. Finishing work like this is time-consuming but not too difficult. However, many electricians are reluctant to agree to this arrangement, since you in effect will be working under their license. If you mess up, they are ultimately responsible, since they are on the permit as the electrician.

In any case, work out any agreement beforehand and have it specified in the contract. If the contractor is using a per-opening figure to bid your job, make sure that he or she adjusts this amount to reflect the work you will do.

HEATING/COOLING CONTRACTORS

If you've lived in a house for a year, you probably have already had reason to call on a heating/cooling contractor for service and repair. Many small remodeling projects don't involve changing your heating system, but a major addition or new house construction demands either modifying or installing heating and cooling systems.

Heating and cooling contractors carry a general contractor's license as well as having someone on staff with a plumber's and electrician's license. They also employ sheet-metal workers who fabricate and install the ductwork used in modern forced-air furnaces, central air-conditioning, and heat pump systems.

For help in finding repair service for an existing unit, one resource is the furnace itself. You'll usually find a sticker listing the emergency service number of a local contractor. In many areas the company that delivers oil is also a heating and repair contractor. If these resources fail, look in the Yellow Pages for a dealer that services the type of system you have. This dealer most likely has the best access to replacement parts and knows the intricacies of your particular brand of unit better than anyone else.

You'll find most heating/cooling contractors also sell furnaces, boilers, and heat pumps. They usually carry a single line or, at best, a couple of different brands. If you have a brand preference you might have only one dealer to choose from for both installation and service.

These contractors will submit a written bid spelling out the exact model numbers and all the necessary components (ductwork, plumbing, and electrical work) to install a new heating/cooling unit or to replace or resize an old unit.

Repair work is usually figured on an hourly rate, which averages $35 plus the cost of the parts. Few contractors give bids on repair work, but most will give you an estimate. Working on older heating and cooling units presents a unique set of problems. A routine maintenance call or minor repair can quickly develop into a major project. If you are faced with such a problem and your house will not freeze up while you contemplate the situation, seek out additional opinions, as most contractors would rather spend the next few days replacing your old unit than fixing it, possibly contrary to what might be most cost-effective for you. If the problem is major and in the boiler, it generally is more cost-effective to put in a new boiler. If it's in the heating unit, often that can be replaced independent of the boiler.

Some contractors offer service contracts for a flat fee. These usually include a yearly tune-up and emergency service. While they do provide peace of mind, they are expensive and seldom pay off. Contractors would not offer this type of service if they continually lost money on them. You are betting it will cost the contractor more to care for your furnace than the cost of the policy, which is equivalent to betting against the house. Contractors don't win every bet, but chances are you'll be paying more often than saving.

If you are acting as your own general contractor on any project that involves adding to or changing the existing heating or air-conditioning systems, you will need the services of a heating or cooling contractor. If you hire an architect or general contractor to run the project, he or she will secure these services. In either case, see that the heating contractor is included in the early planning stages.

The heating contractor should determine whether your existing furnace is adequate, and, if it isn't, the appropriate size of a new heating/cooling plant. This contractor should work with you or your architect to plan and specify carefully the location and size of all heating/cooling ducts or wall/baseboard radiators. If additional ductwork or piping is needed, it should be done while the walls are open and accessible. Installing ductwork in an older house can be a major challenge and therefore a major expense.

If you are hiring the contractor for a remodeling project, check references. Many contractors are experienced in installing heating and air-conditioning equipment in new construction, but lack the experience and creativity to work ducts or run new hot-water pipes into an existing space. Look for a contractor who is experienced in residential remodeling.

Most new houses have forced-air systems. If you have a hot-water system with either radiators or baseboard converters, make sure that the contractor has a hydronic engineer on staff. These specialists design heating systems that use hot water.

Many commercial or apartment buildings have steam heat systems. If your house has this antiquated type of system, consider replacing it. Before you allow a company to work on it, check that it has experience working with this type of system and has steamfitters (plumbers experienced with steam pipes) on staff. The outfit that has maintained your system is a good place to start looking for one of these specialized contractors. Most large heating contractors in and near urban areas have qualified personnel.

Much of the work that heating/cooling contractors do requires considerable skill. The best area for you to get involved in is the demolition and removal of the old furnace, boiler, ducts, or other components that have to be replaced. Have bids prepared in two ways, one with the contractor doing the demolition and installation and another for the installation work alone. The difference is what your labor will be worth to remove the old equipment. Don't forget that it might be a major hassle to haul the old furnace or boiler away unless you have a truck. Old boilers are heavy, and furnaces and ductwork are dirty and bulky. Few garbage services will pick up this sort of trash.

If you have an old heating system in which asbestos was used to wrap the pipes, don't consider doing the demolition work. Asbestos is considered a dangerous toxic material and proper precautions must be taken in its removal, handling, and disposal. Asbestos should be treated by a company licensed to handle and dispose of hazardous waste. Contact your local building department and environmental agency to find out who in your area can do the work.

SECURITY SPECIALISTS

Years ago we didn't have a security specialist in our neighborhood, we had the local locksmith. Today with the growing concern for safeguarding our homes against intruders there are contractors who specialize in the installation and maintenance of security systems. You can take the traditional steps to deter burglars by installing heavy-duty locks on doors and windows or go one step further and use technology to create an electronic fence around your house.

Security specialists install and maintain commercial and residential security systems and should have a general contractor's or home improvement contractor's license, depending on your local requirements. The systems can range from simple hard-wired or wireless perimeter systems that alert you when a door or window is opened to sophisticated motion- and heat-sensing systems that sound an alarm and summon help when an intruder approaches your home.

A good portion of the cost of electronic systems is the installation. It is easier, and therefore less expensive, if the security system is planned and installed during construction, rather than as an afterthought.

Before you call a security specialist, do some thinking about what you want to protect. Try to determine the objective of the system. Why are you considering installing a system? Do you have a valuable collection or keep large amounts of cash in the house? The answers to these questions allow the security specialist to better understand your concerns and come up with a system designed to accomplish your goals and that you can live with.

Your architect or other design professionals that you might be working with can also be helpful in clarifying your needs. There are many areas of overall house design that can affect security. For example, bright exterior lighting at doors and windows is a strong deterrent to intruders. So is the trimming of bushes and trees close to the house, which, left unpruned, could conceal an intruder or provide access to a second floor.

The overall goal of a functional security system is to have it go unnoticed and operate only when there's an intruder. Whether the sensors are hard-wired or surface-mounted, they should be installed so they're not visible at first glance. The control panel should be installed in an accessible area of the house, yet in such a manner that it's not an eyesore.

After your initial consultation with a security specialist you can expect to receive a written estimate specifying the system components and installation costs. If you receive a lump-sum bid, ask for the particulars of the system and a list of customers who've had that particular system installed. Call the customers and see if the system has lived up to their expectations. Ask them if it's easy to live with the system. Remember, a security system that is difficult to operate or overly sensitive can be such a nuisance that eventually it will go unused.

The installation of a basic wireless perimeter system includes sensors at doors and windows to detect intruders, a central control panel, and an alarm. To have such a system installed in a typical three-bedroom, one-story house runs about $2,500. Many wireless systems can be homeowner-installed, so you might inquire into the possibility of purchasing the components and a plan and doing the installation yourself. This could save half the cost of having a system.

FIREPLACE/WOOD STOVE SPECIALISTS

Traditionally fireplaces and stoves were vented into masonry chimneys. These were built by masons, some of whom specialized in building fireplaces. With today's nonmasonry chimneys and zero-clearance fireplace systems that can be encased safely inside wood framing, it is possible to build a fireplace or chimney system without a mason.

Since no heavy masonry chimney is needed, it is possible to install a zero-clearance fireplace or build a chimney for a wood stove where the cost or weight of a masonry chimney would be prohibitive. If a fireplace is high on your list of "must-have's" for your new house or renovation project, then you will probably be installing one of these units. Your best source for expert advice is a dealer who specializes in the sale and installation of this type of fireplace or stove. You can find these dealers listed in the Yellow Pages under "Fireplaces and Stoves-Wood." If you are consulting with an architect or general contractor, he or she should have experience with a fireplace/stove dealer and can recommend someone or include the fireplace installation in the overall bid. The architect or general contractor will then be responsible for seeing that the unit and its installation meet all building codes.

If you are acting as the general contractor or plan to do the installation yourself, you will be responsible for insuring that what you purchase is approved by the local building codes and that it is installed according to code. If you have a particular brand preference, consult the local dealer that carries it. Most fireplace and stove manufacturers have franchised dealers that cover an exclusive area. They can sell you a unit, make the installation, or recommend an installer, who should have a license. Expect to spend $1,000 or more for a stove. If you have a two-story chimney and a double-lined pipe is needed, that figure can double. To have a stove installed, you'll spend upwards of $200 on labor, depending on how much work is required.

Many large home centers and some lumber yards stock a line of fireplaces or stoves or will order them for you. You can even purchase a fireplace or stove and all the accessories needed to install it through major mail-order retailers or from the stove manufacturers themselves.

Building codes are very specific about stoves and fireplaces and their installation. Check that the particular type and make of unit you want to install will meet your local codes. Just because it is sold in your area does not necessarily mean that it is an approved type. Also check on the specific requirements as to the type of chimney and clearances required between the unit, chimney, and anything that is combustible.

Since there is no stone or brick work required, carpenters do most of the work installing zero-clearance fireplaces or wood stoves. Many general contractors do this part of the job themselves. Zero-clearance fireplaces are not difficult to assemble but proper installation requires more than just assembly. To have one installed runs about $2,500. Unless the chimney runs up the outside of an end wall, it must penetrate the roof. The hole must be flashed correctly or there is the potential for a leak. If you are building an addition or reroofing is part of your renovation project, then the roofer can flash the new chimney when the new roof is installed.

Most installers will give you a written bid. It should specify the model (part number) and chimney type (single-, double-, triple-walled). Ductwork should be installed to bring air for combustion to the fireplace from the outside. This ductwork should include a damper control. You can hire a carpenter or even install this type of unit yourself if you follow the specifications exactly. In either case, check with your local building department to see if a specific inspection is required before you can enclose the unit behind drywall.

In some areas of the country you may find building codes that restrict the use of zero-clearance fireplaces or nonmasonry chimneys, or you might prefer a masonry fireplace. In this case you should contact a masonry contractor who specializes in fireplace construction.

Most masonry contractors build chimneys on a regular basis, but not all of them are experienced at building fireplaces. Check their references by asking to see examples of their work in former clients' homes or other locations. This is especially important if you want a unique fireplace built out of stone or one with an unusual design that requires masonry skills and artistic talent.

4

House Interiors

■■■■■■■■■■■■■■■■■■■■■■■■■■■

When you open your doors to contractors you'll be surprised to see they bring a tremendous amount of things with them. This includes their equipment and tools, and is, of course, necessary to getting their job done. To help you prepare for the various kinds of invasion, we have grouped together in this section the contractors who are likely to work inside your house.

Some of these jobs overlap. It is not uncommon for carpenters who work for a small general contractor to staple up insulation, hang drywall, or install a ceiling. You might end up hiring some of these contractors directly or they might end up working as subcontractors for the general contractor running your remodeling or construction project.

Since these contractors come into your house, they will affect your daily routine. Believe us when we tell you that you will get to know some of them pretty well because you will see a lot of them. This section should help you find a good, reliable contractor for interior jobs and give you some idea about how to plan for their arrival.

PAINTERS

Most painting contractors do both interior and exterior painting and some do commercial and residential work as well. In this section we are going to deal with hiring a painter to work inside your house.

Since the start-up costs of getting into the painting business are considerably less than some other trades, there are many first-time or part-time painters around. When you shop for a painter, it makes sense to look for someone who has been in business for a few years and has earned a list of happy customers.

A contractor who is a member of the Painting and Decorating Contractors of America (PDCA), a professional association which provides education and product information to its members, is likely to be versed in current trade practices. However, there are many good small contractors who choose not to join organizations.

Most people have hired a painter at one time or another, so you will not have to ask many friends or neighbors before you come up with several recommendations. Other sources, such as advertisements in the Yellow Pages and local papers, will turn up a long list of potential contractors. Depending on the requirements of where they operate, painters either work under a home improvement or general contractor's license issued by their local municipality.

Most painters buy their painting supplies from a wholesaler who carries several lines of paints. If you have a particular brand of paint you prefer, that brand should be specified in your contract. Otherwise, the contractor will use paint that's priced right and gives good results.

In determining what paint to use, ask several contractors what they would use and why. Ask how they plan to go about preparing surfaces. How much wall patching is needed? Will one coat of paint be enough coverage?

If you ask different painters to give you a price on painting a room you might get three very different bids. Painting a room to some contractors means just that, applying paint to the walls. To others it means careful preparation followed by two coats of top-quality paint.

Individual contractors favor certain brands and types of paints and these are the ones they recommend. Sometimes it's because they get the best deal on a particular brand, other times it's because of the paint's good performance. The price difference between quality paint and cheap, low-quality paint is usually offset by the superior performance of good paint. The cost of paint will represent only about 20 percent of the total estimate. Make sure that you specify you want a top-quality paint—that doesn't, however, mean that it has to be a national brand. Many paint stores that sell to professionals have a house brand made by a major paint manufacturer. These top-quality paints come in plain five-gallon pails.

The labor used to apply the paint will be your major cost. It takes the same amount of time to apply paint that will last three years as it does to apply paint that will stand up to only one washing.

Unless you are willing to do some research about the contents of your paint, you are going to have to take the word of the painter that good-quality paint is being used. Reading the label is not much help unless you're a chemist. One indication of quality, however, is on the paint label where it lists contents. Better paints have a high—30 percent or more—percentage of pigment and resin binder (solids). Your best assurance is to specify in the contract that top-quality paint be used and to choose a painter you trust.

Most contractors figure their jobs on a square-foot basis. They'll measure the room (or eyeball it) and then determine how much preparation is required. For example, to paint a ten-by-fifteen-foot room might cost about $150. The price goes up as the condition of the walls and ceilings deteriorates or when more than one coat of paint is specified. Painting elaborate molding and trim in contrasting colors is another cost escalator because it involves more precision trim work, which takes more time.

Write down what you want the painters to do, and use this list as a specification sheet for each contractor to use to prepare an estimate. You might have to call back some of the contractors you talked with early on and have them submit a new estimate if your plans have changed at all. Having each contractor submit an estimate on the same specifications is the only way you will be able to compare the estimates fairly.

Painting is very labor-intensive. Take painting a typical dining room, for example. Before the painters arrive you should remove all your dishes, glassware, and china from the buffet and china cabinets. The painters move the empty furniture to the center of the room or to a nearby room. They remove all draperies and window treatments, drapery hardware, wall ornaments and pictures, and area rugs. They should spread drop cloths over all the furniture and the floor to protect them from paint spray.

With the walls and ceilings cleared, the painter can begin patching where it's needed. Typical minor repairs include filling in unwanted nail holes and patching minor cracks in plaster walls and nail pops in drywall with spackling compound. The patched areas are left to dry and then sanded. A final coat of spackling compound is applied and again sanded when dry.

If there is serious damage to the walls, much more time and effort will have to be spent to make repairs. Sometimes it might be necessary to have the walls repaired by a plasterer before the painters arrive. For that, you must contract the work out separately.

Before painting begins the painter should dust all the ceiling corners and moldings and along baseboards to remove dirt. Priming is needed in all areas where the old paint has been scraped off and bare wood is exposed. Woodwork should get a wipe-down with a deglosser or be lightly sanded.

Most of the time one coat of latex flat paint on the ceiling and walls and one coat of enamel on woodwork and trim is all that is needed. Two coats might be required if the walls or ceilings are heavily patched or when covering yellow or a dark-color paint with a lighter shade.

The benchmarks of a good paint job are walls that have a flat, evenly applied coat of paint with no visible roller nap marks or telltale repair work. On woodwork and trim where enamel paint meets wall paint there should be an even cut line. On windowpanes the paint should be cut into the joint of the glass and frame, but not spilled out over the glass. All paint should be scraped from the glass. Old windows should not be painted shut, but opened during painting so they operate freely when the paint has dried.

In your discussion with the painters and in the contract you sign, make it clear that you will hold them responsible for any damages or spilled paint. Also ask to see the painters' insurance binders. No matter who paints your house—a one-person operation or a contractor with a crew of employees—they should have worker's compensation along with a liability policy. This insurance is for your protection; without it, you could have a hard time recovering for damages. If the painter drops a bucket of paint on your living room carpet, and is not insured, and does not personally have $5,000 to replace the carpet, you may not be able to recoup anything.

As you can see, painting a room involves a lot of detail work, so there's ample opportunity for you to save some money if you supply some of the expensive labor. If the contractor's estimate is out of reach or you just want to do some of the work yourself, here are some of the jobs you should consider doing yourself:

- removing all furniture and wall treatments, electrical switch plates, and fixtures
- washing dirt and grease from windows
- trimming, patching, and sanding damaged walls.

Just make sure that when you get bids, the contractors are aware of the work you'll be doing so they don't include it in their estimates.

Another option is to have the contractor do all the flat surfaces like ceilings and walls and then paint the trim yourself. Painting windows and doors is time-consuming work that you can do after having the large surfaces done professionally.

Don't take it personally, but if contractors refuse to work with you this way they've probably got a good reason. In the past they may have been disappointed by homeowners who promised to have their end of the job done by a certain deadline. When the contractors showed up the work was shoddy and had to be redone or wasn't even completed. Be honest with contractors and show them an example of your work and probably you can come to terms.

DECORATIVE PAINTERS

Custom-painted finishes, such as a stencil border outlining a room or a faux marble finish on a fireplace mantel, give a room a distinctive look. Faux or fantasy finishes create a special effect that can be as subtle as a soft pastel paint glazed over a darker shade or as dramatic as wood graining on walls to make them look like paneling. Some other popular painted treatments are sponging or ragging a wall with color to give it texture and interest.

Artists specializing in decorative finishes charge upwards of $2 a square foot. The variables for this process make it difficult to estimate an average cost. A wood mantel transformed to look like marble could run anywhere from $300 or more. If this seems expensive, keep in mind that it's custom work and should be compared with having an expensive wallcovering hung. The cost of having a wood mantel painted so it resembles marble is far less than having it replaced with the real thing.

In major metropolitan areas you'll find a good selection of artists who specialize in decorative finishes. They get most of their referrals through interior designers. In less populated areas you'll find their business cards posted on bulletin boards and in paint and art supply stores. They often work for contract designers who do commercial work like designing new restaurants or renovating large buildings.

Those artists specializing in residential work will come to your house for a consultation to talk about what you want and then prepare an estimate for the decorative painting you decide on. Some will prepare a rough sketch if, for example, it's going to be a custom stenciled border. They should also have a portfolio of photos of previous jobs they've completed.

Most of these artisans base their estimates on the decorative painting only. Stenciling, marbleizing, and other decorative finishes are applied over a base coat of paint. The decorative painter will tell you exactly what the base coat of paint should be for his or her particular medium, but most of the time you are responsible for either hiring a painter to apply it or applying the base coat of paint yourself.

How long the entire job takes depends on the decorative finish. Techniques like stenciling and ragging can be rather straightforward, while something like wood graining or marbleizing can involve many more steps and drying time required in between each step. This is custom work and by its very nature will take time.

PAPERHANGERS

Decorating a room with wallpaper is one of the fastest ways to change its appearance. Today's wallpapers are called wallcoverings because they can be made of anything from traditional paper to vinyl-coated paper or fabrics and other, heavily textured materials. To hang such a wide variety of wallcoverings successfully the professional hanger should have experience.

You can't always find paperhangers listed in the Yellow Pages because many of the better ones are kept busy by referral work and don't need to advertise. To find paperhangers, look for their business cards tacked up on the bulletin board at your local paint and wallpaper stores. Or call on painting contractors, who often have paperhangers on their crews.

Some paperhangers are self-taught, while others have gone through a training or apprentice program. One such program is sponsored by the U.S. School of Professional Paperhanging. Local labor unions also have apprentice programs, and completion of these programs allows painters or paperhangers to call themselves journeymen or mechanics.

Unless you live in a metropolitan area, most of the paperhangers you come across will be nonunion workers. An affiliation with a professional group usually means a paperhanger has enhanced his or her knowledge and skills by attending training sessions. The self-taught hangers can also be very good if they have been in the business a long time. In most communities a paperhanger is required to have a business license; in some areas either a general contractor's or home improvement license is also needed. In any case, ask for referrals and make sure the referrals are customers who have had paper hung that's similar to yours. This is important, especially if you are going to invest in expensive paper. You do not want to hire a paperhanger who will learn at your expense how difficult it is to hang a $40 roll of foil wallcovering.

Most paperhangers charge per roll of wallpaper, with an average rate of $16 a roll. For example, in a room requiring eight rolls, the charge would be eight times $16, or $128 for the job. The paperhanger is always responsible for measuring the job and telling you how many rolls are needed. Armed with this information, you'll have a good idea how much the project will cost as you peruse the wallpaper books. If the wallcovering you want is heavy or embossed, or if patching and sizing the walls is required, the cost will be higher.

If there's wallpaper on the walls that must be removed, most paperhangers charge an hourly rate anywhere from $8 an hour up. Removing wallpaper is not a favorite job of most paperhangers, so their charges will reflect that fact.

You can look at wallcoverings at any store, but talk to the paperhanger about ordering what you want. He or she often has access to discounts from wallpaper distributors. If you already have the wallpaper or plan to buy it from a mail-order or discount source, make sure the paperhanger knows this. Have a sample of the paper available when the paperhanger comes to measure. He or she needs to know what the wallpaper is made of to choose the appropriate adhesive. The paperhanger will also want to know that there's enough wallpaper available for the job (and so will you).

In the overall scheme of decorating a room the wallpaper is the very last thing to go on the walls. That means that you have to coordinate the job so that all patching and painting are completed before the paperhanger arrives. The entire room should be cleared and no other work should be going on. The paperhanger will come in with a table, ladders, buckets, brushes, and a pocketful of small cutting tools. The best working conditions are in a room that's as empty as possible of furniture, with bare walls. All wall fixtures, drapery hardware, and electrical switch plates have to be removed. Also remove window treatments or blinds so they're not damaged by dripping wallpaper adhesive.

There is really no way you can work with a paperhanger but you might be able to save some money if you do the preparation work of removing the old wallpaper and applying the wall sizing. This should all be worked out beforehand.

Do-it-yourselfers can successfully hang wallpaper in bedrooms and living rooms. With practice they can move up to more complicated rooms like bathrooms and kitchens. If there's any doubt in your mind, remember that the cost of the wallpaper is usually much more than the labor charge. Don't risk ruining expensive wallcovering. We know more than one person who has had to call in a professional after botching a job. That usually means more money spent on additional wallpaper. If the scope and complexity of the job is risky, like hanging wallcovering in a two-story stairwell, by all means, call in a paperhanger, who has not only the expertise, but also the scaffolding and equipment needed to get the job done safely.

PLASTERERS

In most parts of the country finding a plasterer is a real challenge, but if you live in an area where there are older homes undergoing extensive restorations, your chances of finding a plasterer are pretty good. Today few, if any, new homes are built with plaster walls.

In most parts of the country, a plasterer is required to have a general contractor's or home improvement license. In large metropolitan areas you can find union plasterers, but in less populated parts of the country there is so little plastering being done that the unions are not active except for large-scale restorations and commercial projects.

Except for new construction, plastering is considered a repair by most building departments and a building permit is not required, but check with your local building department.

If you need extensive restoration work done on plaster cornices or other decorative moldings, you can usually find a plasterer who specializes in this. Your local historical society or historical preservation group will most likely have a list of plasterers or one of its members will usually know someone who is still doing this type of work.

Repair work is often done along with other remodeling and construction projects. If you have a water-stained ceiling and call in painters they may tell you that the plaster must be repaired before it can be painted. In this case the painters can probably recommend someone to make the repairs.

There are also professionals who specialize in small repairs like ceiling patching. You can usually find these people listed in the local newspaper under "Building Trades" or "House Remodeling." Drywall contractors and some carpenters will also patch plaster, but most of the time they will want to remove the bad sections of plaster and replace the area with drywall. Many large painting contractors, especially those in cities where there are many older buildings, have a plasterer on their crew.

You might have to do a little hunting, but there are plasterers or at least tradespeople who can repair plaster. When hiring any one of these professionals you should expect to receive a written estimate for any major work, and whoever hangs the drywall should have a home improvement contractor's license. On small repair jobs, few tradespeople will prepare a written estimate. The average hourly rate for a plasterer is $30 an hour.

As with most repair jobs, each contractor or tradesperson will have a slightly different approach. Just remember that if your plaster is loose enough to move when you push on it, a simple spackling job is a waste of money. Carpenters and drywall contractors will recommend the total removal of both the plaster and lath and the installation of drywall. Others might recommend a combination of removal, patching, or laminating drywall over the old plaster. Each way has its merits, but what you should be concerned with is that the proposed work yields a repair that is not visible and will last. After your initial meeting with the contractors you must decide which one presents the best solution to your problem.

Most of this type of work will require demolition and removal of the old plaster. You can do this part of the job and save some money, but make your intentions clear when you are soliciting bids. We have also found that if you have a small patch job, you're better off doing the job yourself. The smaller the job, the more expensive the work becomes. The contractor must cover setup, travel, and cleanup time which might add up to more than the actual time spent repairing your wall or ceiling.

DRYWALL INSTALLERS

Whether it's called drywall, Sheetrock, or gypsum board, the wallboard panels hung on the interior of most buildings is installed by drywall contractors. In most cases they work as subcontractors. They have skilled workers who hang or install the drywall and others who finish and tape the joints. Other tradespeople, especially carpenters, also hang and finish drywall. Painting contractors can usually patch or repair small problems with drywall.

Except for very small jobs and repairs, drywall contractors will supply a written estimate. They usually base this estimate on the number of sheets of drywall that must be hung and finished. To prepare the bid, the contractor should measure the room or area to be covered to determine how many sheets are needed. An average charge for the material and labor is $25 a sheet.

Drywall panels measure four feet wide and come in eight-, twelve-, or fourteen-foot lengths. They are available in several thicknesses. The most widely stocked are ⅜ inch, ½ inch, and ⅝ inch. One-quarter-inch-thick laminating board is also available for installation over existing plaster or drywall. Building codes specify a minimum thickness of ½-inch-thick wallboard for residential use.

The panels are nailed or screwed into the framing lumber. Special adhesive along with either screws or nails is also used. Drywall screws are widely used in commercial construction since steel framing has become common. We prefer that drywall be glued and screwed to the framing. However, this is a slower process than nailing, so some contractors go with nailing. Either way will produce a good-quality job if done properly. If you have a preference, make sure you specify it in the contract.

Some contractors' bids include the cost of the drywall, nails or screws, finishing tape, and joint compound. Others bid on just the installation and finishing of the board, and you must supply the wallboard. These contractors will usually suggest where you can find the best deal on the drywall. Make sure each bid is for the same job so all parties are bidding on the same specs—for example, ½-inch drywall glued and screwed to the framing, finished and ready for paint.

If you end up ordering the materials, make sure you get a price quote that includes delivering the panels to the jobsite. Drywall is very heavy, cumbersome, and difficult to maneuver up a winding or narrow stairwell. When you take delivery, check to see that the board is not damaged, especially along the edges and corners. If it is, refuse shipment.

The key to a quality drywall job really begins with the carpenters, plumbers, and electricians. If the framing is not straight and there is not proper backing in the corners or along the ceilings, the drywall hangers will have a hard time hanging the board.

If possible, have the drywall installer come by and take a look at the framing before you sign off on the rough carpentry. One trade loves to leave work for the next, and each of them blames the previous tradespeople for a bad job.

All electrical and plumbing work must be inspected before the drywall is installed. Don't allow the drywall carpenter to start before these inspections have been made and all work has been passed.

A quality drywall installation shows no seams and has clean, sharp corners. Do not accept work that has craters (low spots or dimples) in the final coat of joint compound. Very small imperfections will be covered by the paint, but any noticeable imperfections should be corrected unless you won't mind looking at them for the life of the addition.

Check to see that the cutouts around all outlets, lights, and switch boxes are not oversized. Check your lighting plan to see that all the cutouts for the recessed ceiling fixtures are actually made. Careless drywallers have been known to install drywall right over openings for recessed light fixtures. Finding these fixtures behind the drywall after it has been installed is the kind of hit-or-miss game that you should not have to play.

Unless you plan to do the entire job yourself, there are not many opportunities for you to work with or do part of a drywalling project. Hanging and finishing drywall is not easy, and it is the most visible part of any remodeling or construction project. It has been our experience that unless you have a small area to cover, you are better off hiring out this phase of your project.

What you should concentrate on is dust control. Finishing drywall is probably one of the worst home improvement projects to live through because it creates so much fine dust. Dust containment can be a full-time job, especially on a remodeling project. Tape plastic across the doors and don't forget to seal off the heating or air-conditioning registers. A forced-air heating or cooling system will quickly clog up its furnace filter and then spread the dust through your house.

CARPENTERS

Carpenters probably put in more hours on building a new house or remodeling project than any other trade. Their duties are basically broken down into two categories, the rough and the finish carpentry. The rough carpenter is the tradesperson madly wielding a hammer, laying out and building everything from the foundation forms to the roof rafters. The finish carpenter, on the other hand, spends most of the time doing detail work like installing windows, trimming with molding, and mounting new kitchen cabinets. They can be the same person, but many times a general contractor will have crews of each.

If you are using a general contractor, then he or she is responsible for finding the right carpenter for the task at hand. If you are hiring a carpenter yourself, then you must try to make a good match. Finding a good carpenter is not easy generally, and finding the right good carpenter to build a set of bookcases or frame an addition is even more difficult.

Most carpenters you hire for remodeling work will probably be skilled in both areas, but if you are going to hire a carpenter to build custom cabinets, then be concerned that he or she actually has experience building fine cabinetry. There are very skilled framing carpenters who seldom get a chance to touch a piece of trim or a cabinet. For the same reason, a carpenter who installs cabinets or does mostly trim work might not be the best choice to build a garage. In rough carpentry the emphasis is on speed at some sacrifice in accuracy, while trim and case work shift the emphasis to precision, with less concern for speed of production.

Since carpenters on most small remodeling jobs do such a wide variety of work it's not surprising that a large majority of small contracting firms are run by carpenters. It's also not uncommon for individuals to pick up a hammer, work for a house builder framing houses for one summer, and then call themselves carpenters. This is not true for union carpenters, who must complete an extensive apprentice program. With such a variety of people answering to the name "carpenter," with varying degrees of experience and expertise, you should investigate the one you are thinking of hiring carefully.

In many communities a carpenter must have a license to contract for work. Some areas require the applicant to pass a test so the license is some sign of competency, but in other communities the license is merely a tax on business. In either case, the carpenter should be able to provide references and show proof that he or she has at least some form of liability insurance, and if he or she has employees they should be covered by worker's compensation insurance.

Check the references. Unless the carpenter comes to you with high recommendation from someone you know, look at his or her work closely. Good carpentry work is neat, with clean cuts and tight-fitting joints. Also ask about the work habits of your prospective candidates. Did they show up on time, clean up, and, most significantly, finish the job on time and within the budget?

Except for a simple repair job, most carpenters will supply, and you should insist on, a written estimate. This should spell out exactly what is to be done and what materials are to be used. Try to insist that a starting date be written into the contract.

Many carpenters and contractors in general don't like these clauses since they all try to take on as much work as possible. Some will tell you that they can start right away or within a week or so, then go into a stall routine after the contract is signed. Make it clear that you don't mind waiting a reasonable time but want an honest estimate of when the work will start.

Even more important than a starting date is a completion date. This date can be your only leverage over the carpenter or contractor toward the end of a project. This clause should also spell out exactly what should be done by both parties if the work is not completed on time. Large commercial jobs usually have clauses that provide for a daily fine to the contractor for each late day. The clause usually awards a bonus to the contractor if the work is completed ahead of schedule.

Large contractors and builders have a team of lawyers to squabble over these clauses. It has been our experience that a more effective method to ensure timely completion is to set up a payment schedule so that the value of the completed work is more than what you have paid the carpenter. He or she is then always motivated to finish the project. The completion date is then a target to shoot for, not an iron-clad guarantee.

Another provision you should attempt to negotiate is one that will allow you to hire someone else to complete the job if the carpenter does not show up and the project drags on beyond a reasonable time. This clause will allow you to apply the remaining money to hiring someone else to finish the job. This is another reason it's important that the pay-out schedule reserves money.

Most carpentry is figured on a hourly basis, ranging from $20 on up, based on the carpenter's skill level plus the cost of the materials. Contractors price their labor to cover their overhead and to pay for the fringe benefits of their workers. In many areas this just about doubles the hourly rate. If you hire a carpenter who does side jobs, you can expect to pay considerably less for the same services. But remember, self-employed individuals have to charge a rate that will cover overhead or they will not be in business for long. Moonlighting carpenters might charge you $15 an hour because they have little overhead and their regular employers are providing their benefits. But beware carpenter contractors who charge $15 a hour when the going rate is $45. A low bid will not look so appealing if the carpenters go bankrupt halfway through the job or you find out the money for your materials has been spent to put a new transmission in their truck.

There are many opportunities for you to work with a carpenter on a remodeling project. You can remove the existing cabinets or knock down part of a partition, for example. Most carpenters will usually be happy to share this dirty work with you. Other tasks, such as nailing deck boards or plywood flooring in place, do not require much skill, except for a strong back and arm to swing a hammer. On many occasions we've been able to work with carpenters, doing the repetitive work they don't particularly want to do.

Trimming a room with molding is the last job to be done by the carpenter. If you possess that skill, it's an area you can tackle. The trim does not have to be completed for the room to be occupied, but remember that every joint will be visible and the overall success of the project is often judged by the look of the trim.

CABINET REFACING CONTRACTORS

Kitchen cabinets are expensive, so expensive that replacing them can be the single most expensive item in a kitchen facelift. Since the doors are the most visible part of the cabinet, they set the style. By refacing only the doors, cabinet fronts, and visible sides you can change the look of your kitchen dramatically. Both wooden and metal cabinets are good candidates for refacing as long as they're sturdy.

This strategy has become so popular that there are people who specialize in refacing cabinets. You can also hire someone to remove the doors and refinish them either with a darker stain or with paint. This approach is generally less expensive than refacing, and you can expect good results if you have good-quality cabinets to work with.

Refacing cabinet contractors will submit an estimate detailing exactly what will be done to your cabinets. Make sure you understand what will be replaced and what stays the same. The more people you talk to, the more input and options you will have.

Personal referrals from friends are your best resource for names of these contractors. In many large metropolitan areas companies actively advertise their services, especially on local radio and in the newspaper. During the initial interview with the estimator who is sent to your house, ask to see samples of the doors, the colors of the finishes, and the hardware. Most contractors will be able to show you before and after photographs of jobs they have completed. The refacing material is a plastic laminate or wood veneer, so you can choose from a wide variety of materials. They also carry a variety of styles of replacement doors.

It's tough to give a ballpark figure for this service because there are no two kitchen cabinets that are the same. However, two rules of thumb seem to apply here: to reface the cabinets in a typical kitchen runs upwards of $2,500, and refacing cabinets is usually half of the cost of replacing them with moderately priced cabinets. Refacing instead of replacing cabinets is also much less messy because the kitchen isn't torn apart.

If your kitchen requires a more extensive facelift and a new floor plan is desired, then contractors can gut the kitchen, remove the ceiling, walls, and windows and rearrange existing cabinets for a better floor plan. While most of their work is refacing cabinets, they can do all the work of a general contractor, adding to your existing cabinets and replacing countertops, appliances, the ceiling, walls, windows, and flooring. They can also make repairs to damaged cabinets. Whatever the extent of their work, they're required to have a home improvement or general contractor's license in most localities.

TILE LAYERS

No matter what home improvement is on your agenda it's possible that you're considering using tile as one of the elements in your project. No longer a mere backdrop for the bathtub or kitchen sink, decorative ceramic tiles splash color on walls throughout the house. A hard-working surface, quarry and vinyl tiles are an ideal choice in sun rooms, kitchens, foyers, and, of course, bathrooms.

Installing ceramic tile on the walls is not exactly an easy job for the average do-it-yourselfer, but it can be done successfully. Laying tile in the foyer can be another story. There is a lot more to a successful tile job than just setting the tile in place. A professional tile contractor can not only install tile but also knows how to install it so it will have a long, trouble-free life.

The professional you hire to install tile is a specialist and should be licensed. Tile contractors, whether large firms or small two-person operators, usually work as subcontractors. You can hire a tile contractor directly or one will be hired by the general contractor running your job. Unless you have heard rave reviews from someone about another tile contractor or installer, you will probably be satisfied with the installer the general contractor chooses.

If you are doing the hiring you should try to match the contractor's experience with your needs. You can expect to pay about $30 an hour for tile installation. Personal references are the best starting point; another is the local tile store. Most stores that sell tile have a list of contractors and installers they do business with. Remember, though, that they are being recommended because they buy tile from the store, not necessarily because they are great tile contractors.

Most contractors, if they have been in business for a while, have experience laying various types of tile. If you are dealing with a one-person operation, find out if it has installed the type of tile you have in mind.

The most important phase of any tile job is the preparation. During your interview ask exactly how the job will be done. What type of adhesives will be used? Most standard tiles can be installed with the thin-set method, using an organic mastic, but some of the larger varieties of tile, like quarry tile, are best set in epoxy or cement mortar. If you are having tile installed on the floor, find out from the tile contractor if the tile can be installed directly on the existing floor. All types of tile need a solid, structurally sound, and smooth base. Find out if a ¼-inch-thick plywood or hardboard underlayment is necessary.

If you are talking with a large contractor with several crews, ask about the specific experience of the installers who will actually do the work on your job.

Check out references when it's possible. Ask to see a job that is similar to what you want done. A good tile job should look symmetrical. The band of tiles outlining the room should be approximately the same size all the way around. There should not be full tiles on one side of the wall and a narrow band of tile on the other. Tile spacing should be even, and the surface should be level. Look carefully at the grout lines; they should be even. The grout should be in the grooves, not smeared on the face of the tiles.

Most contractors calculate the cost of installing or "setting" tile using a square-foot cost. To prepare a quote the tile contractor will measure the area, check the condition of the surface to be tiled, and then decide on the type of installation required. The biggest variables in a tile job are usually the preparation work and the cost of the tiles.

When comparing different proposals it is necessary that all the contractors are bidding on the same type of tile and the same amount of preparation. Listen to the recommendations each contractor gives as far as the prep work is concerned. If most of them recommend that the old floor has to come up and underlayment be installed, then don't accept a lower bid from a contractor who claims the tile can be laid over the existing floor.

It costs about the same to install standard white four-inch square tile as it does to set expensive hand-painted tiles. The cost of the standard tile and labor are roughly equivalent, but if you choose an expensive hand-painted tile the cost of materials will rise sharply. Choose the tile before you get bids on the job, but when you are talking with the tile contractors, listen to their recommendations because some types of tile work better inside or on walls. For example, glazed tiles can be slippery if used on the floor, while some very porous tiles can absorb water and crack if installed outside where they are exposed to freezing conditions.

Many contractors who do small jobs like bathroom facelifts will do tile work as well as setting the fixtures and installing the vanity cabinet. Your agreement should spell out exactly what will be done.

Each tile job is slightly different and unless you decide to do the prep and tile work yourself, your opportunity to do some of the work will vary, depending on how much preparation is needed.

To help you decide how much you want to get involved, here's how a typical kitchen floor installation will go.

Installing tile will put the room out of commission for a minimum of two days, usually more. Preparation begins by removing all the furniture, then the baseboard molding is pulled up and removed. In most cases tile cannot be installed over an existing floor. A plywood subfloor is usually installed. This might involve putting down underlayment-grade plywood, a process that can take a few hours, or ripping out the existing floor and then installing the underlayment. This is time consuming and labor-intensive and a good place for you to get involved.

The job begins with the layout that centers the tiles on the floor so there's an even band of tiles around its perimeter. Some tiles will require cutting to fit exactly to the configuration of the room. The tiles are then set in adhesive which has been spread over the subfloor with a notched trowel.

The adhesive usually cures and sets overnight. The next day grout is mixed, applied, and set in place. Before the grout dries, it is washed off the tiles and pressed into the grooves, making neat, smooth lines. Sometimes a wet rag or towel is dragged across the tiles to smooth the grout lines.

If you're having a custom job installed, like an accent wall of mosaic tiles or a sweeping mural pattern, you'll need a detailed sketch of the wall drawn to scale. The installation is like one of those paint-by-number kits, with each tile set in its proper place. Because the tiles are on the wall your household can continue using the room, unlike a floor job, but there's still a mess because the grouting compound can run down the wall, requiring protective drop cloths.

If you want to work with the installer, the best job you can do is prepare the surface for the tile. For a bathroom that might mean removing old tile or wallboard and replacing it; for a porch or sun room floor it could involve removing the existing flooring (when necessary) and doing the cement work or carpentry required for a new subfloor.

If you're a seasoned do-it-yourselfer you should have no

trouble with the work. If you're inexperienced you'll have trouble convincing the installer you can do the job correctly. A tile installer can't cover up a bad prep job. If the wall surface or subfloor is uneven or the corners are not square, the job cannot be done, so be honest with yourself and with the tile contractor about working together.

RESILIENT FLOOR LAYERS

Sheet goods have been around for a long time. In fact many people still refer to just about any type of flooring as "linoleum." Today sheet flooring and tiles are available in a variety of materials, vinyl being the most popular. The sheet goods are available in long rolls up to twelve feet wide. This allows many rooms to be covered with a single sheet or for large rooms to have a single seam. The flooring is much more flexible than earlier versions, making it easier to install; however, the majority of sheet goods are still installed by professional floor layers.

Flooring installers are usually subcontractors who work for stores that sell sheet goods and other flooring and are required to have a home improvement or general contractor's license to operate in most areas. You can expect to pay about $4 a square foot to have a seamless resilient floor installed professionally. However, that doesn't include the cost of replacing the subfloor or doing any additional preparation work. Floor installers are usually the last subcontractors to come in on a job. Finding someone to install sheet goods is usually not much of a problem, since almost every place that sells flooring also provides installation.

Flooring is sold by the square foot or square yard. If you know the dimensions of the room, you can get a rough idea of the amount of flooring you need and how much the material will cost by visiting a flooring outlet. Unless you are having the floor installed on a new plywood subfloor, you should have someone come to your house and look at your old floor. Don't buy any flooring until you find out whether you need to remove the existing layers of flooring and whether a new subfloor or underlayment is necessary. The answers to these questions will substantially affect the cost of the installation job.

Have the flooring salesperson or installer measure the room. Then he or she can make recommendations about which way the flooring can run so there's a minimum of wasted material. Consider all the recommendations. If one of the flooring installers says the old floor should be removed and another says that the new floor can go over the old, find out why. Just make sure you are talking about the same type of flooring material.

The installer may be a carpenter who specializes in flooring or someone who has been trained at a manufacturer-sponsored training seminar. He might have received on-the-job training by working as an apprentice or helper. In any case, if the installer is working for the store it usually will stand behind the installation. If the installer is recommended by the store, then you should ask for references and check them. Sheet goods are not cheap, and installation techniques vary from brand to brand. Your best bet is an installer who has attended a training seminar or installation school for the type of material you purchased.

If you have an older house with several layers of flooring, the best way for the do-it-yourselfer to participate is to rip up the old flooring. Most installers want to lay underlayment over the old floor, but this can complicate things, locking appliances into their existing places and causing clearance problems with doors. Sooner or later someone will have to strip the buildup of floors down to the original. If that has to be done, you can save a bundle by doing the work yourself.

A typical new kitchen floor installation causes a good deal of disturbance throughout the house. Everything that was in the kitchen must be moved out or, when that's not feasible, moved to the end of the room not being worked on. Try to schedule the preparation work for removing the old floor or installing the underlayment on one day, followed by the installation on the next. If you're working in several rooms, then plan on moving the furniture from one room to another as the project progresses.

Planning the layout of the floor takes considerable time. The pattern of the material should be centered in the room so it has equal borders on all sides. This is especially important if it's a bold or large pattern that will look unattractive if it's not correctly placed. If it's a large room where seaming is required, the seams should be in an unobtrusive part of the room, not in a prominent area.

The large sheets are first rough-cut to fit the room. Some installers make a pattern of the area first and use that to cut the sheet goods to shape.

The sheets are then set in place with adhesive and trimmed to the contour of the projections in the room, like the outside wall corners and door jamb moldings. The material is laid down and any seams are welded together with special adhesives. Finally, either wood or plastic baseboard molding is glued or nailed in place to conceal the gap between the floor and the base of the cabinets and appliances.

If the installer wants to deliver the new flooring material before the installation day, make sure you have a safe, dry place for it. Don't plan on moving it yourself because sheet goods come in long cumbersome rolls that are difficult to handle; floor tiles are sold in boxes which are extremely heavy to lift and move.

FLOOR SANDERS/REFINISHERS

Wood floors have made a comeback and become a selling feature for many homes. Consequently there's probably more than one floor sander/refinisher listed in the Yellow Pages in your area. Another source of recommendations is the suppliers of wood and parquet flooring. These tradespeople work as subcontractors and have a combination of both residential and commercial clients. In most communities they must have a home improvement or general contractor's license. Their residential clients are usually builders who hire them to install and finish new wood floors and homeowners who want their old floors refinished. Floor sanders also make repairs to damaged floors and patch in areas with new floorboards. They have high-caliber equipment and specialized tools for sanding beneath and behind radiators.

A typical floor sander/refinisher contractor will have a crew of several full-time workers and will hire on additional help when needed. Getting an estimate from floor sanders is quite simple and straightforward. They'll come to the house to examine the floors and give you an estimate on the job. Floor refinishing is figured by the square foot. Typically, to sand and refinish a hardwood floor costs $1.40 a square foot. Since labor is the single largest component of the total cost, the more involved the sanding, finishing, and repair work required, the costlier the job.

Ask to see examples of the sanders' work. If, for example, you have an old pine floor to refinish, ask to see their work on a similar floor. A quality floor job should have the finish applied evenly and thoroughly to all areas of the floor. There should be no swirl marks left by the small hand-held edge sander or the drum sanding machine. Door thresholds, closet interiors, and under radiators should be sanded and finished to match the room.

At best, floor refinishing is a three-day affair. Most refinishing involves three sandings with the drum sander: first a sanding with a coarse paper, followed by a sanding with medium-grade paper, and finally a light sanding with very fine abrasive paper. In between each sanding the floor is vacuumed. The final sanding prepares the wood floorboards for a finish, which is usually two applications of penetrating oil or two coats of polyurethane.

To prevent dust and grit from spreading throughout the house, insist that the room be protected with drop cloths to contain the dust within the room. If there is someone in your family who has allergies, has difficulty breathing, or is pregnant, check with your doctor to see if the person should move out of the house. The windows should be opened so the grit and fumes don't remain concentrated.

The refinishing units can also be rented by the do-it-yourselfer.

CARPET INSTALLERS

Most installers work directly for carpet retailers, who handle installation when you purchase carpeting from them. They have their own people install it or subcontract the work. In some instances carpet installers also lay resilient flooring and floor tiles.

If you are going to hire your own installer you might find carpenters or other professionals who can lay carpeting, but check their qualifications carefully and see that they are licensed before hiring them. Installers usually learn the skills on the job when helping an experienced installer. Most of them are not highly paid, so there tends to be a big turnover, especially in large cities where there is a ready pool of semi-skilled workers.

Most installers probably won't have a long list of referrals since they will have done most of their work for a store or flooring outlet. They should be able to explain to you what needs to be done and how they will do it. The best way for you to judge experience is on how knowledgeable they sound when you discuss the job. Ask how they plan to handle a seam if you have a wide room. How do they plan to negotiate the stairs? What about padding, thresholds, and other details, like where the carpet will meet other surfaces? How will they handle the carpet at baseboard heating convectors or around radiators and other protrusions? These questions will at least alert the installer of the potential problems that will have to be faced on your particular job.

Most will quote a square-yard cost for installation and then charge extra for detail work. The going rate is anywhere from $3 to $5 a square yard. Most installers charge an additional $6 per step. Working carpet around stair balusters is usually extra. Get everything in writing, including who will supply the materials.

To judge whether an installation is properly done or just mediocre, do some careful canvassing of a job offered as a referral. Look around the walls and at door jambs where the carpeting is attached. The carpeting should lie flat and not bunch up where it is stapled or tacked in place. Look across a long expanse of carpeting to see that it lies completely flat. There should never be a buckling of the carpet or its padding.

The best area for you to get involved is in the preparation of the room. You can remove the base shoe molding from the perimeter of the room, then pull up the existing carpeting. Prying up the old staples or tacks is easy but time-consuming, making it a perfect task for the do-it-yourselfer. You could also renail loose floorboards or install underlayment if the carpet is to be laid over a concrete floor. If you do any of this labor-intensive work, you might be able to save a good part of the total installation cost.

CEILING INSTALLERS

A prefinished suspended ceiling, a plank ceiling system, or acoustical tiles can go a long way to improve a room. Many home renovation and improvement projects are topped off with a new ceiling system. In fact, this can be the crowning touch in a basement remodeling job or the solution to a noise problem in a home office.

We are going to lump suspended ceilings with acoustical tile since the materials are basically the same. Only the installations are different. Both types are usually installed by carpenters or tradespeople who specialize in ceiling work. There are also ceiling contractors, but these businesses usually concentrate on commercial work. If you want to install a 1,500-square-foot suspended ceiling, one of these contractors will probably give you an estimate, but few will be interested in installing a ceiling in your family room.

Besides a strong personal reference, probably your best source for finding a good ceiling installer is through home centers, lumberyards, or stores that sell ceiling materials. Most outlets for these materials also provide the installation or at least have a list of carpenters who will install a ceiling. Whoever you hire, check first to see that they have a license. Remember that the contractors and tradespeople on the list are there because they purchase materials from the store and not necessarily because of their outstanding workmanship.

You should definitely talk to several carpenters or ceiling installers. You probably have a good idea of what you want, but each of them may come up with some worthwhile suggestions. There are always new products coming on the market, and one of them might provide a solution to a problem like low headroom in the basement or high humidity in the bath. The more installers you talk to, the better informed you will be. Also check the information you receive in the store about the particular ceiling system with the installer. What looks good on paper might not be the best answer to your needs.

It is also important that the installers take a look at the existing ceiling. Unless they know what condition it is in and what obstacles they will have to work around, it's difficult to give an accurate estimate. The ceiling you plan to cover with the new one might be so structurally unsound that it should come down. Water pipes and heating ducts are a challenge in a basement room. Such obstacles as these have to be taken into account for the installation estimate to be valid.

Contractors and carpenters usually charge for installation by the square foot or on an hourly basis. A typical rate is between $15 and $20 an hour. The square-foot and the hourly estimates should be close. Be wary of the carpenter who claims that the ceiling will go up in an afternoon when everyone else has bid the job for two days.

INSULATION CONTRACTORS

Remodeling carpenters install some insulation, but insulation subcontractors usually install insulation in walls, ceilings, and floors. These subcontractors come to the job after the framing is complete and the plumbing and electricity have been roughed in, but before the drywall goes up.

The general contractor will hire an insulation contractor (who is required to have a license) as a subcontractor. If you are running the job you can find insulation contractors listed in the Yellow Pages. Since insulation is a commodity like plywood or two-by-fours, an insulation contractor makes a buck by getting the job done as fast as possible. A standard rate ranges from $15 to $20 an hour. A good contractor can work fast and also pay attention to details. On small jobs your carpenter contractor will probably be willing to install the insulation.

When it comes to remodeling or retrofitting insulation into existing buildings, experience and sometimes ingenuity are the key ingredients. There are many ways to retrofit insulation, and you should talk to as many insulation contractors as possible to get their advice. This is not an easy project, and unless the contractors know what they are doing, you will not receive the full value of the insulation. It may even cause structural damage to your house. The key issues are: What type of insulation is best? How will it be placed in the walls, ceilings, and floors? How will you know that the cavities in these areas are full? Will installing this insulation cause damage to the building, and if so, how much? Who will repair the damage?

Except for factory training and workshops detailing the installation of specific insulation products, most insulation contractors get their experience on the job. While installing insulation is not difficult, studies have shown that unless it is installed correctly, the full benefit of the insulation is not realized. Stopping air infiltration and letting the walls "breathe" are as important as the insulation itself. This is accomplished by careful fitting. Another important component of insulation is the vapor barrier. The more carefully this is installed, the more effective the insulation will be. A proper insulation job is complete when all voids are filled. It also looks neat.

If you have a new house or an addition to insulate, you can price-shop over the telephone, since insulation and its installation is figured by the square foot. Fiberglass is probably the most widely used insulation material in new residential construction, so all you need to know is the total square footage to be insulated. Most insulation contractors will give you a cost per square foot over the phone but will not give an estimate without seeing your job. There are many variables, such as ease of access, that will affect the time it will take to install the insulation.

Installing insulation is labor-intensive, so if you do it yourself you can save money. You'll save the most on small jobs like tucking insulation into the small nooks and crannies of old walls. Contractors will charge you higher rates for this work because they don't want to send the truck and workers out for a low-profit job. You'll probably do a better job, taking the time to work the insulation into every corner.

5

Exterior Projects

■■■■■■■■■■■■■■■■■■■■■■■■■■■■■■

If first impressions are as lasting as people say, then the home contractors who work on the exterior of your house just might be the most important ones you deal with. In this section we will give you a rundown of what to expect when you contact contractors who work on the exterior of your house. These tradespeople handle a variety of improvements and maintenance jobs around the house; they include roofers and painters and the people who install gutters and downspouts or aluminum siding. They also include contractors who build decks, garages, and other such additions.

Many of these improvements are big-ticket items, so the time spent doing investigative shopping is well invested. The more questions you ask contractors about the materials and techniques they plan to use, the more you will know about the job, and the more you know, the better you will be at finding contractors who know what they are talking about. After talking to just a few contractors, you will be surprised to learn how much you can pick up. You won't learn to be a mason by talking to one, but you can find out quite a bit about what is wrong with your chimney. Use the knowledge you gain from talking to one contractor to question others more closely. The answers you get to these questions could save you thousands of dollars.

HOUSE PAINTERS

Most of us have seen the neighborhood Cinderella, the ordinary house transformed into the extraordinary with the whisk of a colorful paintbrush. What's not always apparent is the planning and preparation that went into the job. A professional painter will tell you that it's the prep work that makes the difference between a short-lived job and one that will last many years.

Most likely the same painting contractors who would paint the inside of your house will also work on the outside, though outside work seems to attract "summer only" painters as well, the college kids and schoolteachers who want to pick up summer work. If your house even looks like it might need a coat of paint, you may have already been approached by someone.

You will probably not have much trouble finding a contractor willing to paint the exterior of your house, but you still will have to do your homework to settle on a good one. There are many opportunities to cut corners and skimp on the prep work and that's not the kind of work that you want.

One of the best methods we have used to find a painter is to watch a crew working on a house. This is the best advertising a painting contractor can have. If you see a painter working on a house, ask the owner if you can take a closer look.

From the curb you can see if the painters protect the shrubbery and plantings with drop cloths. If they are working on a two-story house, do they have scaffolding and other equipment that will help them work better and faster? Are they neat? Have they splashed paint on the roof, sidewalks, or other areas?

You need to get up close to see if they are doing a good job at preparation. Are they washing the house, scraping off all the old loose paint, and priming all bare wood spots? The paint should be applied evenly without visible lap marks, brushstrokes, or drips of paint that have dried in place. Look for even cut lines where two different-colored paints meet.

Look carefully at the second-floor preparation. This is the area where it is tempting for the contractor to shortchange the prep work since few homeowners will climb a ladder to check it out closely. If you don't like ladders, check this area from the ground through a pair of binoculars.

Use these criteria when you talk to potential contractors. Their answers to how they will solve your particular painting problems should give you some idea of their knowledge. For example, ask how they plan to prevent the paint under your eaves from peeling. Find out what they will do to get the paint to stick to the wall under the bathroom window. Most such problems are caused by moisture, so don't be surprised if some painters tell you that there is little they can do to keep the paint on the wall if you don't trim back the shrubs or fix the gutter.

Through these discussions you'll probably find out there are two ways you can go—the less expensive minimum quick-scrape one-coat paint job or one involving down and dirty preparation and possibly two coats. Each has its pros and cons, expense being the major factor. Quality paint work, like most other skills, does not come cheap, but it generally pays off over the long run.

Remember, you are not comparing like products if you take

an estimate from a summer painting contractor who uses college students and one prepared by a full-time painting contractor. The college painters could do excellent work; they also might not, and they won't be around to guarantee their work come fall. A painting contractor, on the other hand, makes a living by his or her reputation.

Don't consider hiring a painting contractor unless he can show proof of liability insurance. Exterior work involves climbing ladders and working from scaffolding, so there is a chance someone will be injured. Check with your local building department to see if painting contractors are required to have a license in your town.

All the work should be described in detail in your proposed contract, and the materials specified by brand name and quantity so you can compare different bids. If the painters submit proposals that differ, choose the one you think is the most comprehensive and have the other contractors resubmit bids to these new specifications. The contract should also specify who is supplying the paint—homeowner or contractor. Unless you have a connection in the painting business, it's to your advantage to let the painting contractor be responsible for purchasing the paint because he usually gets the best deal. As a regular customer who buys a lot of paint, the contractor is most likely to have a discount greater than any homeowner could get.

Unless you have a particular brand of paint you want the painters to use, go with their recommendations. Be aware, however, that environmental concerns are causing paint technology to change. In many areas of the country, especially in Western states, the use of traditional oil or alkyd-based paints is being restricted. Latex paints are improving and soon will be the standard. Old rules of thumb favoring oil-based paints outside are slowly changing. Make sure, however, that any paint selected for an outside job contains an algicide. Discuss the options you have in selecting paints with the contractor and find out exactly what he or she recommends.

If you find that two contractors recommend different products and you can't make up your mind, call a large paint store and ask what type of paint they would recommend for the particular situation. Remember, in most cases preparation also determines the longevity of the paint job, not just the type of paint. Consider the preparation, primer, and top coat as a system. Each should be compatible with the other and the painting contractor should stand behind the entire system.

Unlike interior painting, painting the exterior of your house has little impact on the comings and goings of your household. All the work is done outside, so the workers are not likely to be a nuisance. That's not to say their selection of radio music will be to your liking, but their physical presence won't be felt as much because they're outside. The paint fumes won't affect you as much either.

If you're interested in saving money and working with a painting contractor, you can divide the work in several ways. You can do all the preparation and painting on the first floor of the house and hire a contractor to do the work requiring ladders and scaffolding. You can do all the labor-intensive preparation work and have the contractor paint all the surfaces. If there's considerable repair and preparation required before painting, you can hire the contractor to do that and then paint at your leisure.

ROOFING CONTRACTORS

If there's one group of tradespeople who continually get bad raps it's roofers. It only takes a few "gypsy" contractors to give all roofers a bad name. But, in fact, most roofers are long-standing businesspeople who have served their communities for years.

Most general contractors have several roofers they have worked with on different jobs and will subcontract this work out. If you are acting as your own contractor or just looking to reroof your house, the best source for a roofer are recommendations from friends or neighbors. We have found several good roofers by stopping at a job where one is working. Copy down the address of the house, then get the roofer's card (if he has one). After the job is finished, go back and ask the owners if they are satisfied. Another reliable source for recommendations is your insurance agent or possibly a realtor.

All roofers can install an asphalt shingle roof but if you are installing a tile or slate roof or want one repaired, you will find the number of roofers willing or able to do the work very small. Roofers who do have the skill to work on slate or tile mostly do commercial work and are reluctant to work on residences. Their advertisements will note the fact that they specialize in slate or tile roofs.

Because the use of asbestos is being banned in most products, a repair to an asbestos cement shingle roof needs the expertise of a roofer who specializes in working with the material. Because the material is being phased out it might not be easy to find replacement shingles for the job.

How long a contractor has been in business is one reliable criterion for judging potential contractors. Most roofers have the skills to install a new, or reroof an existing, asphalt shingle roof, but inferior work will soon put even the best-talking roofer out of business. We have also found that bids for roofing can vary widely; it is not unusual to receive estimates where one bid is twice another. Don't look just at price; consider the reputation of the contractors and quality of the materials they use.

The best time to talk with a roofing contractor is before you need a new roof. If you have a roof with curling or cracking shingles, shiny areas where the mineral granules have worn away, or a telltale leak, begin the preliminary work of establishing a budget and deciding the type of roofing material you want.

Any roofer you hire must have either a general contractor's or home improvement license and proper liability and property damage insurance and be able to show you up-to-date proof of it. You take a big risk letting someone crawl around on top of your house, tearing the roof off. Just picture your roofer sliding off the roof as a summer thunderstorm hits. He's on the ground and the rain is pounding down on your ceilings. Not a pretty picture.

In addition to having insurance, the contractor should guarantee the work. All manufacturers guarantee their products. Standard-grade shingles might be warranted for ten to fifteen years, while top of the line fiberglass-backed shingles might have a warranty of thirty years. The manufacturer's warranty covers only the material and provides for replacement but not for the installation. Most of these warranties are also prorated, so that if the shingles fail after ten or fifteen years you get only a portion of the cost of new shingles returned. None of these warranties cover faulty installation, so don't expect the shingle manufacturer to be of any help if the roofer does not install the shingles correctly. When the roofing contractor says he or she will guarantee the work, ask exactly what that means— find out what is covered and what is not and have it put in writing.

Roofing is figured by the "square," or 100 square feet. You

can figure that to have a good-quality shingle roof installed you'll pay about $140 per square, and anywhere from $40 to $300 a square for the shingles. On most reroofing jobs the cost of the roofing material will be the major component of the total cost. The most widely used and least expensive roofing materials are asphalt composition shingles and fiberglass shingles. The next most expensive are wood shingles, followed by concrete tiles, and, finally, the most expensive, clay tiles and slate.

The quality of shingles is measured by their weight. Generally, the heavier the shingles, the thicker they are and the longer they will last if properly installed. Standard three-tab asphalt shingles run from about 215 pounds to over 300 pounds a square. Fiberglass shingles are slightly lighter. Fire resistance is also an important factor. A Class A fire rating from Underwriters Lab (UL), an independent testing organization, is the highest, and unless the contractor can convince you otherwise, insist on this class of shingle. All work should be clearly specified in the estimate, along with the brand name, weight, and fire rating of the shingles to be used.

Other factors will influence the cost of your job. If there are two layers of shingles already on your roof, most building codes will require that these layers be removed, as your roof isn't designed to carry the excessive weight of many layers of shingles. The existing decking plywood or boards (the wood between the rafters and shingles or tiles) might be rotten or warped and need to be replaced. Old or warn flashing (the sheet metal covering the joints between the roof and chimney or walls) might have to be replaced.

There is a lot more to roofing than just nailing down the shingles or tiles. For the most part, you are going to have to rely on the integrity of the roofer since it's difficult for the average person to judge a roofing job from the ground, or even if you climb up a ladder for a closer look. Before you make the final payment, however, you should check that the shingles or tiles are laid in straight, evenly spaced rows. They should lie flat, without any noticeable waves or bumps. It's also generally considered better to "weave" shingles between the pitches of two roofs than to use flashing. It makes a better water seal.

Unless you decide to do the entire job by yourself, there are few ways to get involved to save money. Removing several layers of old roofing is very labor-intensive, but remember, it means working on the roof, which is unfamiliar and uncomfortable territory for most of us. Another problem in doing part of the job yourself is that once the project begins, it should finish quickly. You might spend days removing the old roof in preparation for the roofer, exposing the interior to the outside. If he doesn't show up, and the weather deteriorates to rain or snow, you have a mighty big problem. When the roofer removes the old roof, he has a crew of workers who can apply the roofing felt and start laying the new roof as the old one is ripped off. In general, we've decided that roofing is one project that we gladly leave to the professionals.

GUTTER/DOWNSPOUT CONTRACTORS

Next to the roof, gutters and downspouts are your house's most important defense against damage from moisture and rot. Through the years, gutters and downspouts have been made from wood, copper, galvanized steel, and now plastic.

If you are looking to replace or repair your gutters, most lumberyards, home centers, and other outlets for gutters and downspouts will give you the names of installers. There are also contractors who specialize in installing gutter systems, but just about any of the trades, including roofers and carpenters, will install gutters on a small remodeling job. The workers you choose should have a home improvement or general contractor's license.

Some contractors specialize in making custom seamless gutter systems. Long rolls of prefinished aluminum are bent to shape on the job by a special machine. This allows the contractor to fabricate a single length of gutter with joints only at the corners, instead of every ten feet as is required of regular gutters.

For aluminum gutters and downspouts, contractors charge about $4 a running foot (a foot of gutter or downspout) for the material and labor. If repair work is required to the wood fascia boards behind the gutter or to the overhanging areas of the roof called eaves, a carpenter may have to be called in.

Insist on a written proposal that includes the specifications for the materials. Be sure to have the contractor specify the gauge (thickness) of the aluminum or galvanized steel to be used. A standard for good-quality aluminum is a minimum thickness of 1/40 inch, and galvanized gutters should be at least 26-gauge. If you receive a bid that is considerably lower than the others, it could be that the contractor plans to use a lighter-weight material.

When you discuss the job with a contractor or installer be sure to point out any drainage problems you have. Show and tell the contractor where and under what circumstances these problems occur. It's possible that the existing downspouts need to be moved. Work these details out before the job starts, since the pitch of the gutters is calculated in relation to the planned locations of the downspouts. Once the gutters are set, it's difficult or impossible to reposition the downspouts. Also check on how the water will be directed away from the house once it is collected, or you may end up with a leaking foundation or worse.

In addition to protecting your house from damaging water and snow, gutters and downspouts should complement the architecture of the house; they should be seen but not noticed.

If you own an older home and need someone to repair or install copper gutters and downspouts, look for similar work being done in other renovations; this costly material requires the talents of skilled, experienced workers.

Also, if your plans for the house include a new exterior paint job, it's easier to do the work (or have it done) before gutters and downspouts are installed.

MASONS

On today's construction site masons do much more than lay bricks. They lay out and supervise the installation of the foundation, footings, and other concrete structures. Later they lay the brick veneer used on many houses or build a fireplace or chimney. In metropolitan areas most of this work is done by union-trained masons who have gone through at least a two-year apprentice program. In areas where unions are not as strong, most masons learn their trade through a less formal training program. In these areas masonry contractors who do commercial work are usually large enough to hire on apprentices. Aside from trade schools, this on-the-job training accounts for most of a mason's professional education.

Since masons work on so many different aspects of construction, it takes a long time for one to become extremely proficient in every area. A mason can work for a large masonry contractor for years and never build a fireplace. Finding a mason might not be a problem (they're listed in the Yellow Pages), but finding a mason with the experience to engineer and construct a brick fence with an arched gate around your patio is another matter. If you're restoring an old house with a crumbling chimney, look for a specialist in preservation or someone with experience working with old bricks (and the inherent problems).

Most masons work as subcontractors and are hired and supervised by a general contractor. If you are hiring a mason directly, it is important to establish his experience and confirm that he has a license. Get references for work that reflects the type of masonry you have planned. If you want an elaborate double fireplace with a raised hearth, don't even consider a mason who can't produce some satisfied customers for whom he has built a similar fireplace.

Estimates should specify the materials to be used. Take bricks, for example. There are many types of brick—common, face, and pavers, to mention a few. Face brick comes in several grades, SW (severe weathering) or MW (moderate weathering). Just specifying red brick for a walk or fence is not enough.

Ask each mason you interview what type, style, and grade of brick is most appropriate for your project. Or if you have already settled on the brick, check with the masons to see if they agree it is appropriate for the job. The choice of brick will affect the overall cost of the project, so you should be familiar with your alternatives. This will also give you an opportunity to compare the recommendations of each of the masons. If you aren't using brick, find out exactly what type of concrete, mortar, stone, or other materials will be used.

A house is only as strong as its foundation, and this is also true for a masonry project. Since masonry is so heavy, a critical part of this type of project is a properly designed footings and foundation system. No matter how pretty the fireplace looks, if it settles even slightly, structural cracks will develop.

If you are planning anything more elaborate than a simple

wall and do not have an architect or general contractor supervising the project, be sure to have the mason prepare a set of working plans that you can take to the building department for approval. Inspectors will then come out and check the footings. This is no absolute guarantee that the foundation won't settle, but at least you will be assured that the footings and foundation meet minimum standards.

A starting date should be part of your written agreement. Additions and most other building projects start with a foundation. Delays at the beginning of a project are hard to overcome since they interfere with the work schedules of the other contractors. Carpenters can't do the framing and plumbers and electricians can't run their lines until the mason has laid the foundation.

Few masons will want to work with an amateur bricklayer, but you could get involved in the project by acting as the mason's helper. You can do the demolition and cart away the old bricks or help move supplies. With supervision you could mix and carry mortar. You could also help carry and erect scaffolding. Talk this all out before you come to any agreement with the mason.

Brick and mortar are messy and can damage landscaping near the house if it's not properly protected by drop cloths or heavy plastic sheeting. Mortar dries to a solid glob of cement that can dig into a tree limb or break shrubbery branches or mess up flower beds. Whether you're helping or just observing the progress of the job, be on the lookout for this type of damage.

DECK CONTRACTORS

With the ever growing popularity of expanding a house into the great outdoors, some carpenters have changed their business cards to read "Deck Contractor" or "Outdoor Designs." Even in cities like Minneapolis and Chicago where the weather is not conducive to year-round outdoor living, these specialists have healthy twelve-month businesses.

You'll find that some large deck contractors can give you a complete design package. They have architects and landscape architects on their staff or work with them on a regular basis. They can build a multilevel deck with sauna and fire pit and do the plantings and terracing, as well. A full-service contractor like this might be your best bet if you have ambitious plans for your deck and yard.

If your deck plans are more modest or you already know exactly what you want, a carpenter contractor who specializes in decks might be exactly the person you're looking for. He won't have the staff, and therefore overhead, of the larger concerns. Whatever the scope of your project, the contractor must have a general contractor's or home improvement license and should also carry liability or worker's compensation insurance.

You can also get design help at most large lumberyards and home centers. They usually have someone on staff who can help you with the design of your deck. Computers are beginning to pop up in these stores to help with this service. Most stores will provide you with a list of materials needed and a list of carpenters who build decks.

Before you start looking for a deck contractor or visit a lumberyard, have a clear idea of how you and your family will use the deck. Also have on hand a survey of your property so there's no question about where your property line runs. A good deck designer will notice the orientation of your house to the sun and point out the pros and cons of different deck locations.

If you have a limited budget for the deck, make sure the

contractor is aware of it. To give you a ballpark figure, expect to spend about $10 a square foot for materials and labor to have a good-quality deck built of pressure-treated lumber.

It's possible to get a long-range deck design that you can build onto every few years. This spreads the cost over a period of years while giving you a well-conceived deck in the long run. Talk about your budget at the beginning so you and the contractor understand the conditions before making elaborate plans that won't be realized.

A deck contractor should know the building code requirements within your locality. These include the depth of the footings, acceptable construction techniques, requirements for railings, and any height restrictions. It will be his responsibility to get the required building permit and see that the deck meets all these requirements.

All specifications for the deck, along with a drawing, should be submitted by the potential contractor. It is important that the grade and type of lumber is specified exactly. The term *pressure-treated lumber* refers to a large group of products, so the specifications must be more detailed—for example, *chromated copper arsenate (CCA) treated #2 or better. Southern yellow pine* refers to a particular type and quality of wood.

Further specifications for redwood and cedar should also be given. The heartwood of these two trees is very rot- and insect-resistant, but the clear knot-free grades are very expensive. *Construction heart* is a grade of redwood that is reasonably priced. Don't be tempted to build your deck from "standard" (#3) or "utility" (#4) grades of lumber. Have the contractor use "construction" (#2) or better. When you compare different estimates, make sure the same grades and types of wood are specified, as the lumber grade will affect the cost of the deck.

While we are on the topic of wood, you should be aware

that there is a debate going on between the pressure-treated wood industry and many consumer groups about the safety of the material. The issues are unresolved, but many communities are giving second thoughts to using pressure-treated wood to build playground equipment, benches, and other public structures that people, especially children, come in frequent contact with (see p. 147).

At this date there is little evidence to show that structures like decks built with pressure-treated wood pose any health risks. If you work with this type of material or are around when your contractor is working with it, avoid breathing in the sawdust (this is true for any species of wood) and don't burn the scraps in your fireplace.

All the contractors should have a list of clients for whom they have built decks. Ask to see one that was built several years ago. The older decks will give you an idea of how the work holds up. The decking boards should be straight and not warped. Look for nails that have their heads driven flush with the surface of the wood—they prevent stubbed toes. The careful contractor should also take the time to drill a pilot hole for each nail driven in at the end of a plank to prevent it from splitting.

The construction of a deck usually doesn't affect the interior of the house. It does, however, make a tremendous mess of the outdoors. A delivery truck deposits piles of heavy lumber in your yard or driveway. If excavation is needed to dig deep footings, a backhoe will be necessary. If it rains, you'll have to deal with plenty of muddy traffic through the house. This is an inconvenience to be sure, but certainly worth the annoyance when you consider how much you'll enjoy using your new deck.

If you want to participate to save some money, consider hiring the contractor to build the foundation. Have the post holes dug and the posts set and the beams leveled: you can nail on the decking. This is very labor-intensive work, but if you can pound nails straight, you can successfully install decking.

SUNSPACE BUILDERS

Serious gardeners have greenhouses attached to their houses so they can nurture their favorite plants throughout the year. A sunspace addition is one step beyond an upgraded greenhouse. This glass-enclosed space is a living space for both people and plants. It made its debut back in the 1970s when homeowners began experimenting with solar additions.

Sunspace additions are made of wood or extruded aluminum with glass or plastic panels. Many are sold as kits that an experienced amateur can assemble. In addition to the kits, there are contractors who specialize in the design and construction or, in some cases, the assembly of sunspaces.

Some of these contractors are general home improvement contractors who have experience in the design of custom sunspaces. They work in wood or they can design a sunspace and assemble it from manufactured components. These contractors can offer you a wide selection of materials and designs from which to choose.

Some sunspace contractors are distributors for particular manufacturers of sunspace components. They will design and erect a sunspace using the brand of components they represent. These contractors purchase the components from a single source, so their designs will hinge around a certain system. Much of their energy will be spent convincing you of the advantages of their system.

In addition to these contractors, there are salespeople who sell sunspaces. They represent the manufacturer and will arrange for the installation of the sunspace through a subcontractor. During your initial contact, make sure you understand the relationship between the people you are talking with and the products they are suggesting you purchase.

To have a sunspace constructed for you will run about $120 a square foot. A typical kit for a sunspace measuring eight by fifteen feet will run about $6,000. Extras include heating, ventilation equipment, and shading and cooling devices.

When evaluating different systems, look for quality materials. This is especially important if you live in areas of the country that receive heavy snowfall. All framing, hardware, and fasteners should be rust-resistant. Glazing material should be safety glass or plastic. Wood framing members should be made of pressure-treated wood or at least wood treated with a preservative.

Since a sunspace is considered a permanent structure, you should consult your building department for the requirements of the local codes. Contractors who build sunspaces are considered general home improvement contractors and most localities require some sort of licensing. In addition to the actual erection of the frame, the contractor will probably subcontract out the foundation, electrical work, and plumbing to a mason, electrician, and plumber. These tradespeople may also work directly for the contractor.

Along with the estimate, drawings of the sunspace and a complete specification list should be provided by the contractor. You might be dealing with several people, the sunspace manufacturer who will supply the parts and the contractor who will erect it, and both should submit complete detailed estimates. If you decide to purchase a sunspace kit, have the supplier provide you with a drawing and specifications so you can get estimates on its construction.

Aside from a direct referral from a happy customer, checking out the contractors' references is the only way you can judge the quality of the workmanship. While you are checking out the work, ask the owners about their experiences with the sunspace and/or contractor. Ask about claims that the builder or manufacturer makes. Does it actually cut your heating bill? Is it usable in the winter? Is it too hot in the summer? Have there been any leaks, or moisture, or settling problems?

As with most products, some are better than others. The best recommendation of both a contractor and system is a sunspace that has lived up to the expectations of the owner for a couple of years or longer.

Basic sunspace kits are not too complicated and can be successfully installed by homeowners with experience in carpentry. Consider contracting out the foundation work and doing the assembly yourself. Or you might consider doing the finishing work, like laying the floor or installing the trim.

GARAGE BUILDERS

In densely populated areas of the country you'll find home contractors who have made a thriving business of building garages. They are in the Yellow Pages and will gladly come out and show you their catalogs of styles and designs. These builders are general contractors who usually have a crew of carpenters and subcontract out the other work. If you live in a rural or sparsely populated area, you won't find a garage builder, but will have to hire a general contractor to build a garage. He or she is required to have a license in most areas. This is a competitive business but as with most other contractors their prices do vary with their work loads.

Garage builders benefit from the ability to purchase materials in large quantities. Some of their savings are passed on to you. They usually offer you the best price on a stock garage—

the key word here is "stock." If you want an oversized garage or one that is completely different from their stock offerings, garage builders lose some of their price advantages.

It's important that the design of the garage fits in with the architecture of your house. Even though it might be slightly more expensive to have a custom garage built to match your house, it is a worthwhile investment. Exterior elements like the roof line and pitch and siding are important considerations. A garage can be freestanding (detached) or attached to your house. A garage addition should enhance the aesthetics of the house, as well as provide security and protection for your car.

Give each contractor a copy of your plot survey so they will know where to place the garage. In many areas of the country banks require a plot survey be done in order for you to obtain a mortgage. If you don't have a plot survey you might go to city hall and check the tax records. There are usually plot books showing your property and its boundaries. The builder can use this plot survey or make his own to prepare the necessary drawings for the city or county building department. The placement of the garage must meet all current building code setback requirements, which state exactly how close the building can be to the adjoining property.

The procedure for building an attached garage is similar to that for a detached one except in how and where the garage connects with the house. Sometimes it's separated from the house by a breezeway, but often it opens directly into the side wall of the house. Opening the existing house wall presents some sticky problems. Most exterior walls are load bearing, so if the contractor has to make an opening for a door, the wall must be properly reinforced. Make sure the contractor checks that there are no electrical or plumbing lines or heating ducts running through the wall in this area. If there are, they will have to be rerouted and this will be an additional cost. Have him check before he submits a bid so there will be no surprises later.

The most popular size garage is twenty-four feet square, large enough to accommodate two cars with some storage area as well. This will run you upwards of $10,000. Other features you might want to include are a workshop area, overhead storage in the rafters, lighting, and an electronic garage door opener. If you plan to use the garage year-round for working on your car or as a workshop, include the cost of insulating the walls and adding heat or air-conditioning. The cost of a custom door, windows, and an electric door opener also runs up the basic price of a garage.

There are many other options to choose among—some garages are prefabricated units while others are custom built. You should establish a style and a list of features when you talk with the first builder. If you need a driveway, make sure to include the specifications for it. The cost of a long cement driveway is almost as much as that for a small garage. Get all the contractors to bid on the same job. If you want to know the cost of additional features, have them listed separately, so you can compare estimates for the same project. Also check that all fees for building permits and bonds are included.

Most of these contractors will be able to give you a long list of referrals. By all means go look at their work. The emphasis of most garage builders is on number of garages built, not how elegantly they're done, so check out the detail work carefully. How the trim and siding fit will give you some indication of how carefully the garage was built. Check the slab for any major cracks or settling.

When a detached garage is being built on your property you'll be well aware of the concrete mixers and lumber trucks delivering materials, but basically the work won't affect the daily life (except for the noise of pounding nails) of your household. It's a different story when an attached garage is built on the side of your house. While the contractor will most likely build the new garage before breaking into the wall, there still comes the inevitable time when your house is opened into the new garage and all its construction dust. Opening the wall and constructing the door should not take more than a couple of days. Insist that the contractor put up plastic sheeting to contain most of the dust.

Garage contractors work fast and have specialized crews, so they are not going to allow you to get in the way. Painting the exterior of the garage after it's built or finishing the interior with insulation and drywall are probably the best projects for you to tackle to save some money.

EXCAVATORS

On most construction sites, clearing the lot, digging the foundation hole, and leveling the ground for a driveway is done by an excavator. This contractor uses heavy equipment, such as a bulldozer or a backhoe. Excavators also remove trees and other growth from the building lot. Most of the time they work as subcontractors, hired by the general contractor or supervising architect.

In most areas of the country an excavator must have at least a business license from the community where he works. In other localities excavators are licensed or are required to have a general home improvement license. Any project short of just digging a hole will also require a building permit.

Finding good, reliable excavators is usually not a problem since they seldom work on a project alone. Excavators are usually the first subcontractors to work on a construction project, so masons and contractors who do foundation work have working relationships with several. We have relied on the recommendations from these contractors because they have to rely on excavators to dig properly in order for their work to begin.

Excavators usually charge by the hour. Their rates vary, depending on the size of the equipment used. The more horsepower a bulldozer has or the larger the bucket on a backhoe, the more it costs per hour. For example, the hourly rate for a bulldozer and operator can range from $100 to $150 an hour.

It has been our experience that excavators who specialize in small jobs like residential foundations don't have a wide selection of equipment. If the excavator does have a selection of equipment, considering hiring the larger machine if you have big hardwood trees you need knocked down. A large machine can do more work per hour. But if your site is small or access is difficult, using the larger machine usually doesn't pay off.

If you are acting as the general contractor, it is your responsibility to see that the excavation is done properly. It goes without saying that the hole has to be dug in the correct location, but it must also be dug to the proper depth. Before you allow any digging to begin, make sure that you know the exact location of all water, sewer, gas, telephone, and electric utility lines. Call your local utility companies well before you plan to excavate; they will come out and mark the locations of their lines. You might consider hiring a surveyor to stake out the lot lines and locate the corners of the foundation.

Once the excavation begins, you have to supervise the excavator. Foundation footings must rest on undisturbed virgin soil; the ground can't be backfilled under the footings. The footing trench or foundation will be inspected before the footings can be poured. If the building inspector finds backfilled earth under the footings, the trench will have to be made deeper. The foundation wall will then have to be made higher to compensate, costing you more money. Make sure the excavator stops a few inches above the final grade. The footing trench should be dug by hand the last few inches by the masonry crew that builds the footing forms.

Your mason might help supervise the excavator. He can come to the site, set up a builder's level or transit, and take depth measurements. Another alternative is for you to rent a level, have them set up the instrument, and show you how to use it. You can then supervise the digging, which is not difficult.

If you can't find help or be there yourself, then hire an excavator who will supervise the digging. Make clear from the start, however, that there will be no general contractor or mason on the job and that the excavator will have to determine and maintain the grade.

Excavators will also remove the topsoil from the area where the driveway and sidewalks will be laid. After the foundation is in and the project framed, the excavator will return and backfill the area around the foundation and do any final grading that is necessary.

Excavators will give you a written estimate that should include a general description of the work. You should check that it includes hauling trash like tree stumps and excess earth from the site and indicates that any trees you want to save will be tagged in red. Also, make sure the contract states that the excavator will be responsible for setting and maintaining grade if he agrees to do this. There should also be a clause that states that the excavator will contact you before he starts work and that you have to be on the site before work can begin.

Pay only for work actually completed. Try to delay payment a few days until the mason arrives on the site and checks out the excavation. If the job isn't done correctly, it might be necessary to do a lot of hand digging which will cost you money. Remember, if you are the supervisor on the job, you control the digging and cannot hold the excavator liable.

Unless you can operate an excavating machine, there is not much you can do to help the excavation work. One area where you can save some money, though, is to clear a heavily wooded lot. You can cut down the trees and save the hardwood for firewood. This will cut down on the amount of trash that has to be hauled away. If you decide to cut the trees, leave large stumps (three or four feet high) so the bulldozer will have something to push against and the excavators can wrap the pulling chain around them when they remove the stumps.

BASEMENT WATERPROOFING CONTRACTORS

Solving a wet basement problem might be as easy as redirecting your downspouts or regrading the dirt around the house. It might also involve backhoes, drainage pipes, and thousands of dollars.

If you have a damp basement, your first goal is to diagnose the cause. Excess moisture in adjacent areas is often the culprit. The challenge is deciding how the moisture gets into the area and then formulating a plan to stop it.

Whom you should seek advice from on these matters depends on the nature of the problem. If you have an active leak in the foundation, then repairs from the inside will seldom do the job. For major problems you're best served by a mason or cement contractor who has had experience fixing foundations.

But many times dampness can be cured from the inside. Here again, a mason who does foundation work is a good bet, but you should also seek the counsel of basement waterproofers. They are listed in the Yellow Pages, but check first with your town's Better Business Bureau as you'll see that basement waterproofers as a group are probably at or near the top of their complaint list. Also check to see that they have a general contractor's or home improvement license.

When talking to any of these contractors however, remember that each has his own case to make. Masons will want to dig up your foundation and get in there to see what can be done, while waterproofers will want to apply sealers to either the outside or inside of the foundation. The real problem is that there is no "best" method to dry up a basement.

Before you consult with a contractor, fix any leaky gutters and downspouts. See that rainwater is directed away from your house. If everything is in good order, then extend the reach of the lower horizontal downspouts that run away from the house. Do minor excavation to be sure that your yard slopes away from the foundation. Then wait and see if these alterations make any difference or perform this simple test—tape a twelve-inch-square piece of aluminum foil to the wall or floor of the foundation. If, after a couple of days, moisture collects on the outside of the foil, then you have a condensation problem. Increased basement or crawlspace ventilation will usually cure it. If there is moisture on the inside of the foil, then moisture is moving through the foundation, usually by capillary action. It's possible to solve this problem from inside the foundation by patching all small cracks with mortar and coating the foundation with a cement-based water-resistant paint. Minor leaking can be stopped by chipping away any loose cement or mortar and then filling the crack with hydraulic cement, which will expand as it hardens to close up the leak.

It's tough to stop an active leak from the inside permanently. Contractors who suggest approaching this type of problem from the outside of the house are probably on the right track. They will want to dig a trench around your house, which can be life-threatening to shrubbery unless it is carefully moved with root balls wrapped in burlap. Sod can be cut away. If it is kept watered, it may be repositioned once the work is completed. With the foundation completely uncovered, drain tile and basement waterproofing is applied to the outside of the foundation. Then the foundation is backfilled and shrubbery and sod are replanted.

When you call in contractors, make them specify what they think the cause of your problem is. Finding the source of excess moisture will usually lead to a permanent cure. Deciding which contractor has accurately determined the cause and has a reasonable cure should be your first consideration. The cost of the work will vary considerably, depending on what needs to be done. Generally, the materials to waterproof a basement are not expensive, but the labor is. This will be the biggest factor in determining the cost of the job.

Get references from your chosen contractor and check them. The older the job, the better. Also make sure that the problems were similar to the one you have. Visiting a job where a coat of cement-based paint was used to cure dampness caused by capillary action isn't going to help you decide if the contractor can stop your major foundation leak.

Many of the cures for a damp basement are rather fundamental, like increasing ventilation and putting down a plastic vapor barrier over the ground in a crawl space, things the homeowner can do. Other cures, requiring digging up the foundation, are best done with a backhoe, but if you are ambitious you could dig it by hand. You might also be able to work with the basement waterproofer and provide some of the grunt labor. Before you commit yourself to this work, find out exactly how much you will save. It does not make much sense to spend a week breaking your back to save a couple of hundred dollars when the contractor's equipment can dig up the foundation in six hours.

WINDOW REPLACEMENT CONTRACTORS

Over 44 million single-family homes in the United States are seventeen years of age or older. With this figure in mind it doesn't seem unusual to see companies advertising replacement windows on TV. There certainly are a lot of potential customers out there.

This large market allows contractors to specialize in window replacement. Most general and carpenter contractors will also be glad to give an estimate on replacing or repairing windows. There are window companies that have showrooms where you can see a broad selection of window styles and sizes. Most lumberyards and home centers also carry a selection of windows and will provide sources for their installation. Whoever you hire should have a license.

You might be surprised at just how expensive replacement windows are. When your house was built, the windows were a major expense, so to replace them today is not a trivial matter. To replace a large old window with a good-quality vinyl clad thermopane can cost $300 or more. If you are considering replacing all the windows in your house, get ready for a hefty bill. There are ways of financing this improvement, but you could also consider replacing one or two windows each year. First you have to weigh the expense against the benefits carefully. If money is not a problem, the convenience of easy-operating, energy-efficient windows is worth any price. But if you look at replacement windows as a money-saving investment to cut your heating bills, it will be a long time before you recover the initial cost and actually begin to save.

The actual value of the labor used to replace a window is

low compared with the cost of a good-quality vinyl or aluminum-clad Thermopane window. Most experienced carpenters will have no trouble replacing a window, so if you intend to do this, direct your research to finding the window that best fits your budget and needs.

There are actually several ways you can go about this, but first check to see if there are any restrictions on architectural modifications to your house. You might live in a historic district or there may be an architectural review board in your subdivision or town that will have something to say about what you can do with your windows. Check with them. They can be helpful in suggesting a style of window that will enhance the value of your house, not detract from it.

When you look at different windows, keep the architectural style of your house foremost in mind. It seldom pays to attempt to modernize an older house by replacing the double-hung windows with more contemporary casement windows. This is especially true for the front facade. That's not to say that a casement window can't be used when you're remodeling; they're an excellent choice for kitchens and bathrooms.

Probably the most economical approach is to have the old windows rebuilt with a jamb liner kit. These kits allow the carpenter to remove the old sash and weight system, then to install jamb liners which provide new tracks for the old jambs to slide in. The old window sashes are cut to fit the new tracks and then reinstalled and weatherstripped. Teamed with a good-quality storm window, this modification produces an energy-efficient window.

Contractors can also install jamb liners and replacement sashes. These new sashes usually contain double-pane insulated glass. This is more expensive but you can gain the advantages of increased energy efficiency and low maintenance from the vinyl cladding.

Replacing the old window with a new one is another option. New top-of-the-line windows are better than old double-hung, or old steel or aluminum windows. A new window can usually be installed inside the old opening with minimal disturbance to the interior and exterior of your house.

Replacement windows can be made of wood, vinyl- or aluminum-clad wood, or solid vinyl, or aluminum. Individual salesmen or contractors representing a particular brand of window or a carpenter who has had experience installing a particular brand will all emphasize the merits of whatever type of window they sell or prefer. There is no one best window for every situation; you have to shop around and ask questions.

A window replacement contract should include the exact description of the windows to be used and the modifications necessary to the existing windows. The estimate should also clearly state in writing how much the contractor will do and how much will be left up to you. Can the interior trim be reused? If not, will the new trim match the old? Who will reinstall it? Who will repaint it? Will there be damage to walls, floors, and exterior siding? Reviewing estimates on the cost alone will be difficult unless all the contractors are using the same type of window and installation.

A bid to rebuild your windows should specify the type of jamb liners and weatherstripping to be used. Make sure that the bid also includes a description of how the old sashes will be repaired or rebuilt.

If you are reviewing several options, look over all the estimates and then decide which approach seems best for your pocketbook and your house. Then take the specs and ask several of the other contractors to resubmit estimates based on the type of window you have chosen. Most contractors can give you a window-by-window cost. The cost per window is higher for one or two windows than it will be for a dozen since it costs the contractor the same to set up.

In most cases replacing windows or renewing old ones is straightforward, and most contractors do a good job and will be prepared to stand behind their work. Your long-run satisfaction with a window replacement may depend on the quality of the windows you choose. As we said before, there is no best type of window, but there is a direct connection between the cost of the window and its long-term performance. Before you choose a contractor, consider the manufacturer's warranty on the windows and the reputation of the contractor.

Most homeowners with carpentry experience can rebuild or replace a window. Unless you want to do this job yourself, there is not much you can do to help out and cut the cost. Removing the woodwork goes quickly and most contractors will probably want to do the whole job themselves. You might get involved with the painting and rebuilding of the old sashes, however.

AWNING AND CANOPY SPECIALISTS

With the developments in synthetic fabrics, awnings have made a big comeback, both in the commercial and residential fields. Fabric awnings and canopies provide colorful and attractive solutions to shading the house from sun and providing shelter.

In most areas of the country there are awning manufacturers that produce stock-sized awnings or do custom work. If you live by a body of water or river you might also look for a canvas shop that makes covers and tops for boats. You can also purchase ready-made awnings from major mail-order retailers. Some large home centers and lumberyards also carry or can order awnings.

Awnings and canopies can be made from aluminum. These can be stock or custom made and can usually be purchased through suppliers of aluminum siding, gutters, and aluminum shutters. Aluminum awnings and canopies are also available from major mail-order retailers, lumberyards, and home centers.

Before you shop for awnings, check to see if your house is in a historic district or if your subdivision or community has an architectural review board or commission. Awnings will change the look of the house, and some of these boards want to see the style and material before they will approve such an exterior addition. Many such boards and commissions publish guidelines; get a copy before your heart is set on a particular style of awning. If you are not under the jurisdiction of such a commission, then check with your local building department to see if local codes impose any restrictions.

Most companies that manufacture or supply awnings will also provide for their installation. Whoever installs the awning must have a license. Some sublet the work, others have their own crews of installers. To get an idea of the cost, figure that you can have a good-quality canvas awning for a single window installed for about $140. This includes the frame, mounting hardware, awning, and labor.

If you buy from a manufacturer or supplier, a salesperson will come to your house to show you material samples and styles. He or she will also take measurements and prepare an estimate. Or you can go to the awning store to look at samples. If you do, it's helpful to have a snapshot of your house to give the awning specialist a good idea of the way it looks.

After you have settled on a material and style, consider the installation hardware. Make sure you understand exactly how the awning will be attached to the house. If it is larger than the window, then the mounting hardware will have to go on the siding. If the awning is the same size as the window, then the hardware must go on the window frame. Don't assume anything. Will the awning interfere with the shutters? Will a brick house affect installation?

Installing awnings and setting up canopies is not too difficult, so when choosing a supplier, look for an outfit that has been in business a long time and has good references. They should be willing to stand behind their product with a warranty. The manufacturer of the fabric will also warrant it against fading and defects. But remember, a warranty is only as good as the people servicing it—a good reputation is really the best warranty.

While you can save the cost of labor by installing an awning yourself, remember that few manufacturers want to hear complaints about faulty manufacturing or materials if you do the installation.

SIDING CONTRACTORS

Whether you're remodeling a house or building a new one, selecting the siding can be an involved process. Unless you're dead set on a particular type, style, and color, you'll be surprised at the choices you have.

In the movie *Tin Men* we all saw a humorous portrayal of the aluminum siding business in the 1950s, when this new and revolutionary material was introduced to the mass residential market. High-pressure salesmen are still working in this business. Vinyl siding has become an even more popular cover-up for houses, but wooden boards, or shakes, and plywood sheeting also make up a large part of the exterior siding market, along with brick and stucco.

Siding contractors usually do other home improvements, like gutter/downspout repairs or installations. If you are work-

ing on a construction or remodeling project with general contractors, they will handle hiring a siding subcontractor, but
most likely they will have their carpenters install the siding.
Since most competent carpenters can install siding, when you
are sizing up the contractors, check their record. Ask for referrals and follow them up. Also contact your local building
department and Better Business Bureau to see if there are
complaints filed against the contractors. Check to see that
they have a home improvement or general contractor's license.

The biggest challenge you will probably face is deciding on
the siding material. Before you get involved in trying to evaluate the relative merits of one siding material over another,
decide on the style you want. Check with your local building
department to see if you are in a historic district or if your area
has an architectural review committee. If there is one, they
will want to know the style and material you will use. Their
major concern is whether the new siding will fit the architecture of your house. The siding is the most predominant architectural feature of a house, so you should give considerable
thought to how it will look as well as to how long it will last.

You might already have been approached by a home improvement salesman over the phone selling siding, windows,
and other improvements. The potential problem with purchasing siding this way is that the purchase is seldom thought
out and is not usually part of an overall long-term plan for
your house. Siding should be one of the last improvements
you make. Consider any other exterior improvements you're
planning on making. If you are planning an addition, kitchen
or bath upgrade, or other changes that might require moving
windows or doors, wait on the siding.

Siding contractors usually figure jobs by the square foot for materials and labor. For example, vinyl siding typically runs about $3 a square foot. The "eaves," the part of the roof that projects over the sides of your house, and the soffits and fascia boards that form the cornice under these overhangs are usually covered with the same siding material. These are usually figured by the linear foot.

The labor charges are for installation only. One of the most important parts of your siding agreement should be the extra labor charges required to prepare your house for new siding and to make any necessary repairs. These could be minimal, or they could involve removing the old siding, replacing rotten sheeting, and rebuilding or replacing rotten window or door trim and fascia boards.

Have all this spelled out in writing. To give you an accurate estimate, the contractor must take a close look at your house and check for problem areas, then decide what should be done and how much it will cost. Another area you should clarify is how the new siding will negotiate windows, doors, and corners, both inside and outside. Have the contractor show you pieces of the trim moldings or at least pictures of it. Aluminum and vinyl moldings can look pretty bad if they are not applied carefully. Make sure you know what the siding job will look like and how all the details will be handled.

A good-quality siding or re-siding job is evident at corners and where the siding meets window or door trim. If the siding looks tight and neat without gaps, it usually is. Even if your house is a little out of plumb, each horizontal run of siding should meet evenly at every corner.

There are plenty of areas you can get involved in on a typical siding job. You can repair all the areas that are pointed out by the contractor and remove the old siding if there is any.

WROUGHT IRON CONTRACTORS

Specialists in ornamental ironwork have been embellishing the exteriors of American houses for years. Listed under "Railings" or "Iron Work" in the Yellow Pages, you'll find these craftspeople do strictly custom work. Like all contractors, they are required to be licensed.

Wrought iron shops do a lot more than make stair railings. They can create a back porch canopy with stairs, a front door railing unit with built-in bench seating—even a freestanding gazebo. They can make any number of fancy fences, gates, window bars, and door guards. They also make stock lengths of standard railing which can be cut and finished to any length.

You'll find a limited supply of ready-made stair and hand railings in large home centers. These are usually of light construction, but they are inexpensive.

If you call a wrought iron shop, they will send out a sales representative, who will bring samples and photographs of their work, to take your order. Some shops maintain a showroom where popular items are on display. You can also look at completed projects that are ready for installation. If you visit one of these shops, bring along a photograph of your house so the sales representative will have an idea of its architecture. The photo will help show exactly where you want the railing or other ironwork installed.

If you are concerned about cost, ask about prices for different styles or sizes right away. The more elaborate the design, the more expensive the item will be. If stairs and railings seem expensive, then you probably haven't shopped for their wooden counterparts. Both are costly. Wrought iron handrails are usually more expensive than wood but an iron railing is usually less than a comparable wood railing, especially when you consider the cost of installation. A typical plain ornamental railing runs about $25 a linear foot installed.

Before you place an order, have the salesperson check your measurements. While he is there, ask how the rail will be installed. If you are having a canopy or other design built, find out how it will be attached to the house. Will the support post need footings?

It is best for the iron shop that builds your creation to install it. This way if something does not fit, the discussion will be between their own employees. It's easy to pass off a slight misfit as faulty installation if there is a separate subcontractor involved. This is more difficult to do if the same shop is doing the installation.

If you are getting bids from several shops, and we suggest you do, settle on a specific design, then have each shop bid on it. If the installation is included, then have all the proposals include the installation cost. Have the style and dimensions included in the written proposal along with a sketch of the finished work. Most shops will have to draw up something to work from, so they usually won't balk at a request for a drawing. Before you award any work, take the drawing and specifications to your local building department and check to see if it meets all local code standards.

Unless you can weld, there is little you can do to help fabricate the ironwork. If you are replacing steps or a railing, you can do the demolition work. You can also do the painting. Wrought iron is sometimes delivered with only a coat of primer on it to help prevent rust. It should be painted soon after installation with several coats of an exterior enamel.

TV ANTENNA AND SATELLITE SYSTEMS INSTALLERS

A TV antenna installation usually involves a lot more than just putting up the antenna. You will find contractors (usually TV repair shops and satellite-dish sales outlets) who specialize in the service and installation of antenna systems. Most stores that sell televisions also install antennas or subcontract the work. If you live near an urban area, you can expect to pay about $200 for a standard television antenna system. This includes a fringe-area antenna, strap mounting on your chimney, the coaxial cable lead-in, and a single TV hookup.

In some areas these contractors must have a general home improvement license, in others no such requirement is necessary; check with your local building department. Whether or not the contractor is licensed, he should be insured. Roof work is dangerous and you want his insurance to protect you from liability. Don't allow anyone to climb on your roof without first showing you proof that he carries liability insurance.

Unless you are contacting the TV antenna contractor for the repair of an existing antenna or a new satellite installation, you should make a list of the problems you are having with your present TV reception. Which channels do you get good reception on and which don't you get at all? What kind of interference do you experience and at what time of day or night? This information will help the antenna contractor access your situation and make a recommendation.

It has been our experience that trying to repair a very old or bent antenna is a losing proposition. Antennas have improved in design, and it will take the antenna mechanic more time to try to repair the old one than to install a new one.

Unless you know about electronics it will be difficult for you to evaluate the contractor's recommendations, so your best bet is to get the antenna contractor to guarantee the good reception of certain stations by contract. But be sure you both agree on what good reception is. It is also to your advantage to talk to several antenna contractors; this way you can compare the recommendations against one another.

The installation of a satellite dish is a little more involved than that of a typical TV antenna because the site selection and alignment are more critical. You might have to trim or remove a tree or other obstruction that might block the signal from the satellite. If you live in an incorporated area like a town, check with your local building department first to see if you can erect a dish.

The cost of the components (dish, receiver, etc.) is the major part of this project, so the quality of the components you choose will have a greater effect on the total cost than the installation will.

The contractor should be able to provide a list of references in your area where he has systems running. This is the best way for you to check his work. By talking to his customers you can also become somewhat knowledgeable about satellite receiving systems. Try to find out how the different systems hold up over the years. If you can, take a look at the TV picture. Check to see that all the satellites you have been told you will receive are actually picked up and have an adequate picture.

Along with the complete specifications of the system, try to get the contractor to put in writing which stations you will be able to receive. If you live in an area where there are trees or other obstacles that might disrupt reception of certain satellites, check with the contractor before you commission the work. You might not want to cut the top of your favorite tree off to improve TV reception.

Another factor that will influence the cost of an antenna system is the in-house wiring. The basic system will include running a wire (usually coaxial cable) to a single TV set. If you have several TV sets spread throughout the house, the cost of wiring them can add up. Ask the contractor if the cable will be run through the inside of the house or strung around the outside. It is less expensive to run the cable around the outside of the house, attaching it to the siding and then feeding it through the walls to the set. Fishing the cable through the attic and then into the walls takes a lot of time. If you don't mind the cable on the outside of your house consider this alternative, otherwise be sure to find out how the contractor plans to route the cable.

If an installation is scheduled for a rainy or windy day, don't be surprised if there's a cancellation; it's not safe to work on a roof in those conditions.

6

The Yard

■■■■■■■■■■■■■■■■■■■■■■■■■■■■■

Gardening is America's number-one hobby; over 75 percent of U.S. households are engaged in some form of it. And there's never been more interest in the environment, especially in your own backyard where you're probably spending much time and money. The basic backyard with a swing set for the kids and folding lawn chairs and grill for the adults is giving way to a yard filled with playhouses, saunas, and gazebos. Chain-link fences are being replaced by elaborate custom-designed enclosures.

The backyard is an extension of your indoor lifestyle, so there's a lot of emphasis on well-thought-out design. Lawns and gardens are full-time passions for many of us, and there's a large group of contractors who specialize in servicing the great outdoors. In this section we'll look at contractors who can help you get the most from your yard.

LANDSCAPE CONTRACTORS

The Oxford dictionary defines "landscape gardening" as "the arrangement and planting of trees, shrubs, grass, etc. on a tract of land." When the tract of land happens to be your yard, this "arrangement" becomes a very personal exercise. The challenge is to make the most of the natural setting and downplay its less appealing features.

The size of your yard is an important factor. Sometimes it's easier to work with an empty acre of land than within the confines of a small city lot with restrictions on all sides. The condition of the soil, how the yard is affected by the sun, and its proximity to neighbors will all influence a backyard's ultimate design and layout. Lest we forget, most of us have budget constraints, too.

Transforming your backyard dreams into reality is the job of the landscape contractors. They excavate, build retaining walls, install underground sprinkling systems, plant gardens, grass, trees, and shrubs—whatever it takes. Most communities require that a landscaper at least have a business license and some also require a general contractor's license. Planting grass and trees and minor excavation usually do not require building permits, but major grading and the construction of retaining walls and sprinkler systems usually do.

Landscaping is seasonal work in most parts of the country, so landscapers hire part-time workers for the summer months. Landscapers themselves go in and out of business frequently, so one indication of a good landscaper is how long he has been in business. Guarantees from a company that goes out of business in the fall will do you little good next spring. Like all other contractors you hire, make sure that landscape contractors have a license and liability insurance that covers their workers.

Because it's so visible, a landscaper's work is easy to judge. You can glean landscaping ideas in new housing developments where landscape contractors showcase their work with the hopes of finding prospective clients. An even more accessible source for ideas is your neighborhood. Don't be afraid to knock on someone's door (at a reasonable time of day) when you notice a landscaped yard that you like. Take a walking tour of various neighborhoods on the weekend, when it's likely you'll find homeowners out and about. There aren't many of them who won't be complimented that you noticed and asked about their yards.

For you to get the most from the services of a landscape contractor, you should have an idea of what you want so he or she can come up with an overall plan. The more detailed your ideas, the better. Some landscape contractors charge a flat design fee based on the size and scope of the job; others offer the design service free when you purchase planting materials from them. Having a plan allows you to spread out the project cost over several years but end up with a well-thought-out yard.

The very least you can expect from a landscape contractor is that the plantings will flourish and thrive in your yard. If any plantings die within a year after they are planted, most contractors will replace them. Make sure you specify this in your agreement. Have the contractor submit a written proposal describing all work, plants, and materials to be used, with any guarantees clearly stated. The contract should have estimates for discrete elements of the design, e.g., "$500—removal of hedging material along the side yard" or "$300—plant dogwood tree in front yard." This allows you to compare different estimates and to decide just what you can afford to do this year and what to put off till next.

In deciding what to have done first, work from the inside of the yard out or away from the house, so that heavy equipment won't trample on newly planted flower beds or delicate new tree roots.

Landscaping is very labor-intensive. If you are willing to supply a portion of that labor, you can save a substantial part of the total tab. You can have the landscaper supply and deliver all materials and do the planting yourself. Another option to consider is to break up the work load. Have the contractor lay the sod and plant the trees, and plant the flower beds and shrubbery yourself. Or have the contractor prepare and sod the front yard and heavy-traffic areas, and seed the rest yourself. The more sweat you put into the project, the more money you can save, but make sure this is all specified up front in your contract.

SHED/OUTBUILDING, GAZEBO BUILDERS

The construction of a storage shed or workshop in your backyard can put unused space to practical use, while the addition of a charming gazebo might add the finishing touch to a lovely garden. Some builders specialize in outbuildings or lawn structures, but often you'll find a deck contractor who builds gazebos or a garage builder who does workshops and sheds. Both must be licensed.

If you have a specific design in mind or have purchased plans from a design firm, you can hire a general contractor or a carpenter to build it for you. Using the design, either can give you an estimate based on the materials specified.

Surprisingly, these structures, while small, are costly to build since the same steps needed to build a house are required to construct a ten-by-fourteen-foot shed. You need a foundation, wall and ceiling framing, siding, roofing, a door, and possibly a window or two. In essence you're building a small house.

Before plans get too far along, check with your local building department to see what code requirements apply. The issues of greatest concern are how far the structure must be set back from your lot lines, its height, and its overall square footage. If you live in a town or suburb with a historical commission or architectural review board, they will want to see a drawing of the structure before permitting it.

Both the zoning laws and building codes must be met before the municipality will issue the necessary building permits. If you are replacing an existing shed or outbuilding, some of these points might not apply, but you will still probably need a permit.

Contractors who specialize in building small outbuildings usually have a good handle on their costs. They will submit an estimate and usually cost out options, like running electricity out to the shed, windows, doors, etc., as flat-fee extras. To have a good quality ten-by-twelve-foot shed made of pressure-treated lumber built on a cement block foundation will cost about $2,600. As you go up in size and options, so, of course, does the price.

When you are getting bids for structures, make sure big-ticket items are of comparable quality. Some contractors build on a foundation of cement blocks, some prefer a concrete slab, while still other use cement-block piers. These foundations are all adequate for this type of structure but there is a big difference in cost. You can't compare an estimate for a structure with a concrete slab with one sitting on four cement-block piers.

Besides the type of foundation, all materials should be clearly specified. Check the quality of the windows when you are comparing estimates. Many times the standard windows included in an estimate are nonopening or of very marginal quality. This is fine if you plan to use the structure for storage only. If it will do double duty as a garden shed or workshop, being able to open the windows will be important.

Another area where these structures might differ significantly is in stud spacing and the use of pressure-treated lumber. Some structures have studs on twenty-four-inch centers, others on sixteen-inch centers. If the codes allow it, either is okay, just be aware that a structure built with joists on sixteen-inch centers will require more wood and is usually stronger. Also, pressure-treated lumber should be specified for all areas that will be closer to or come in contact with the ground. Check to see if sheeting is to be used under the siding; this will make the building sturdier.

An alternative to building the structure on-site is having a prefabricated unit brought to your lot and put on its foundation. Some units have foundations of pressure-treated wood that can sit directly on the ground, so no masonry foundation is necessary. This approach eliminates some of the construction delay problems normally associated with inclement weather. You can construct the foundation or hire a mason to do it when the weather permits. This way the building crew can pick a nice day and build the shed. It also lets you see the exact structure before you buy it. One drawback is that these units cannot usually be tailored to suit your specific needs. What you see is what you get.

Prefabricated units can be purchased in a variety of ways: delivered and installed on the site, delivered on-site ready for a do-it-yourself installation, or strictly as an off-the-lot item that's ready for pick up by someone with a truck and trailer-bed rig.

There are plenty of areas for you to get involved. Why pay

someone to clear the site of shrubs, trees, and other obstacles? The shed or gazebo must be protected from the elements, so paint or stain it yourself. Consider finishing off the inside of your new shed with insulation and shelving. With a new gazebo in your backyard you can tackle the landscaping around it yourself.

FENCE CONTRACTORS

Aesthetically, a picket fence around a Cape Cod or a brick fence surrounding a Colonial can be a wonderful finishing touch. Fencing around a yard serves many purposes—it keeps kids and pets safe within the confines of your yard, it can partition off a swimming pool, and can increase the security of your house.

Since fencing contractors are usually carpenters or builders who specialize in designing and building fences, they are required to have a license. You'll find they do a wide range of custom design work. Some fencing contractors deal exclusively with chain-link fences, but the biggest share of that work is in the commercial market. For residential use, chain link is popular for enclosing dog runs or swimming pools. Wood, especially cedar and pressure-treated wood, is another frequently used fencing material. The shape and design of a custom-designed wood fence is only limited by your imagination. Split rail, stockade, picket, and lattice fences are but a few styles you can choose from.

If you want a stone or brick wall built, you will probably have to deal with a fence contractor who will subcontract the work to a mason. If you have a pretty good idea of what you want, you could hire a mason directly.

Before you decide who will build your fence, contact your local building department. All localities have some restrictions on fencing. Some limit the height of residential fences while others, especially in historic districts, have jurisdiction over style and material. How close a fence is to property lines, streets, and roads is also usually restricted. Check the limitations before you get too involved in planning the project.

You must positively identify your property lines before digging any post holes. Your local city or town office might be able to give you a copy of the tax map that would show your lot and property dimensions. Better yet, consult the survey that you probably received when you purchased your house. Check this out carefully, as there is not much you can do if five years from now the fence is discovered to be three inches into your neighbor's yard when he tries to sell his house.

The biggest advantage of dealing with fence contractors is the wide variety of fence styles they can show you. Their experience will help you decide what type of materials and style is best suited for your house and lot. Some contractors maintain showrooms so you can see a selection of different types of fencing. This is especially helpful when you don't know exactly what you want. These contractors can also send you to former clients with houses or lots similar to yours so you can see the actual fencing.

If you can't decide between fence styles, get bids on each style you're considering. When the estimate for the cedar basket weave fence comes in at three times the estimate for a split rail fence, the split rail might begin to look pretty good to you. After you have looked over initial estimates, finalize the fence design and then, if there's been a change, have contractors resubmit estimates. In general, fencing is sold by the running foot. A pressure-treated board and batten fence constructed on-site runs about $10 a foot; for a chain link fence, it costs closer to $7 a running foot.

The written proposal should specify the length, height,

shape, and design of the fence, along with the materials to be used. The type and grade of wood, nails, screws, and other hardware should be clearly spelled out. How the fence posts are to be anchored in the ground and other general construction specifications should be included.

You're not likely to find a fence contractor willing to let you work with him on the job. On the other hand, many dealers that install fences will sell you all the materials you'll need to build the fence yourself and will deliver them to your jobsite (and give you some good building tips, too).

The site preparation for the new fence is one area you can get involved with to save some money. If you have a flat landscape with no obstructions, there isn't much to do. But if the property along your fence line needs to be cleared of overgrown brush and weeds, you can tackle that part of the project. You might want to have the fence contractor estimate how much the site clearing will cost so you can decide whether it's worth the effort. It's always good to know exactly how much your labor is worth.

SWIMMING POOL BUILDERS

The ultimate dream for some homeowners is a backyard swimming pool. While an aboveground pool can be successfully installed by the do-it-yourselfer, an in-ground pool of gunite (a concrete mixture sprayed over reinforced bars) or a pool with a vinyl liner is definitely a project for a pool contractor.

An in-ground swimming pool is a hefty investment, costing upwards of $15,000. If you are thinking of having a pool built, the first thing you should do before you contact a contractor is to establish a budget. Remember that in addition to the initial cost of the pool, you will have to maintain it over the years.

Check with your local water department about the cost of filling the pool with water. Are any special taxes levied on pools in your area? What are the local requirements for fences? What about restriction on size, depth, and materials?

The more you know about the code requirements, the better informed you will be when you talk to the contractors. Their recommendations will have to be tempered by this code, and if they start to promise things you know they can't deliver because of local restrictions, a warning flag should go up in your mind.

Look at your future pool as just one of numerous features that will make your backyard more usable. To get the most enjoyment out of the pool, carefully consider its location and how it will work with the other areas of your yard.

Swimming pool contractors are listed in the Yellow Pages and are only too happy to send a salesperson to your house. Your biggest challenge is to get the salesperson to translate your ideas into concrete or vinyl, not just to try to sell you what he has.

Some contractors can design and build a pool using several different systems, while others deal with a single pool supplier. The single-product contractors will champion only one type of pool. If they represent an aboveground aluminum-walled vinyl-lined pool manufacturer, for example, then they will press this type over all others. For this reason try to get proposals from as many different sources as possible. Don't rule out an in-ground pool because you think it might cost too much. You may find a slightly smaller basic in-ground pool is not much more than an above-ground pool with all the accessories.

Listen to the sales representatives and weigh the advantages of one type of pool over another. If an in-ground vinyl-lined pool sounds appealing, talk to someone who owns one.

These contractors should be able to provide you with references. You can check out their workmanship and possibly see the pools. If you visit one of their showrooms, take along a snapshot of your backyard with its rough dimensions.

In the swimming pool construction business, the longer a contractor has been in business the better. Except for a very basic aboveground pool installation that requires no plumbing or electrical work, a pool contractor will either have to have a licensed plumber and electrician on staff or subcontract out this work. In most areas, pool contractors are required to have a general contractor's license. Since word-of-mouth recommendations make or break these specialty contractors, you should shop for a licensed contractor with a good reputation.

Where you want a pool and where it can actually be built are not always the same spot. Your local building codes have requirements and the condition of the soil plays an equally important role. Excavation is costly, so you want to avoid digging into ground that's rocky and filled with boulders. You also need to know where your water, electric, and sewer lines run. If they're in the wrong place they can be moved, but that's expensive.

Get estimates that include the entire package, not just the construction of the pool. Additional items include ladders, diving boards, filter system, heater, pool cover, lighting, and decking. Have the estimates itemized so you can decide which options to include in the contract and which to add on later.

It is important for your contract to state that the pool will meet all local building and health codes. Each municipality has its own codes and you want to be sure that your pool meets every requirement. Most areas require fencing around the pool, and the contractor should know the type and size. The filter system and plumbing must also meet all local codes.

PLAY STRUCTURE BUILDERS

Yes, there are even contractors who build jungle gyms! In our age of special interest magazines and cable television networks, it's not surprising to find such a specialized service. These contractors offer the complete service of designing and building play equipment on your property. They will also design and deliver the system for you to install.

You'll find several listings under "Playground Equipment" in the Yellow Pages; these companies deal primarily with businesses, schools, and parks. Some also market to homeowners. There are also companies that sell and construct kids' play equipment specifically for the home market. If they don't have a listing in the telephone book, you might find them advertised in the "home" section or Sunday magazine of your local newspaper.

You're not likely to find these contractors in small communities, but you can hire a carpenter to build or erect play equipment if you purchase a basic design. Most lumberyards and home centers have plans that include part lists and complete assembly instructions.

Contractors who specialize in this type of work are usually required to have a general contractor's or home improvement license. They will give you a package price on one of their stock designs. Modifications to a stock plan or a custom-built unit will usually be contracted out on a time-and-materials basis. If you hire a carpenter to build a unit, expect to pay anywhere between $20 and $30 an hour.

Some communities require a building permit to erect just about any structure. Some suburban communities have an architectural review board and may require you to submit the plan for the play equipment. In either case, if you hire someone to build play equipment, make sure that he gets the necessary permits.

Regardless of who does the job, it should be designed with safety in mind. Some indications of a good design include extensive handrails at child level, ladders and climbing posts that are railed, and slides with high side guards. All surfaces should be smooth and splinter-free. Edges should be rounded, and all hardware or fasteners should be recessed below the surface of the wood.

Most often, play equipment is made of cedar, redwood, or pressure-treated wood. Some use a combination of wood and heavy-duty plastic and rubber. A typical setup has a swing, a slide, and monkey bars. More deluxe versions feature gym rings and seesaws, hand-over-hand bars, a tower climber, and a fort that's either open with a canvas canopy or enclosed with a door and roof.

Some communities are rethinking the use of pressure-treated lumber for public playground equipment. The toxic chemicals in pressure-treated wood might pose a health hazard to children if they come in contact with the wood on a regular basis. At this time there is little evidence of this, but the cost of redwood or cedar will not substantially increase the cost of your playground equipment. You might also consider building the framework of the setup out of pressure-treated wood and using redwood or cedar in all areas that your children will come in contact with.

You can work with contractors or manufacturers in two ways. You can buy the equipment from them and have it delivered for you to build, or you can commission them to build it. Since many of these structures can be erected in modular form, it's possible to begin with a basic setup and add onto it as the children grow up.

7

Specialty Service and Maintenance Contractors

■■■■■■■■■■■■■■■■■■■■■■■■■■■■■

Keeping a house in shape is akin to keeping your body fit—it takes year-round vigilance and everyday sweat and perseverance. While we all know the benefits of maintaining a house, it doesn't just happen by itself. In this section we'll look at the contractors who perform maintenance services.

We limited this section to contractors who don't perform routine services. Most of you are familiar with appliance repair people, so we tried to include services you might not be aware of—one-shot services that you will use occasionally, not on a regular basis.

EXTERMINATORS

Unwanted bugs and crawling creatures can be a real nuisance. Insects like termites can literally eat your house, while pests like squirrels that invade your attic can make you crazed as they chomp away on your electrical wiring. Getting rid of these critters before they do damage and preventing their return is not easy. In fact, it's big business, and there are major companies with thousands of people in the field every day doing battle.

Even though these exterminators and pest control companies are found in all parts of the country, they usually are not immediately called in when a roach or flea is discovered. Hardware stores and supermarkets have shelves full of bug sprays, mouse traps, and other pest-killing devices. Sometimes a persistent homeowner armed with these off-the-shelf pesticides is all that is needed to control the pests found around the house. However, there are times when the homeowner loses the battle and should turn to the professional for help.

Exterminators can be found in the Yellow Pages in most towns and cities around the country. Since these contractors disperse toxic chemicals, all states require certification (though some allow noncertified personnel to work under the supervision of a certified operator), and some require licensing. Don't consider doing business with an exterminator who is not certified. Some exterminators specialize in certain aspects of the business, such as termite control. Other large outfits have experienced personnel who specialize in all areas of pest control.

These contractors charge by the job, their fee based on time and materials. A typical 1,000-square-foot house runs about $150 for a flea bombing and a follow-up treatment. The prices will vary according to the size of the house and the extent of the infestation.

Before you contact an exterminator, try to assess your problem as best you can. If you have a roach or flea infestation, try to remember when you first noticed the problem and pinpoint the affected areas. For a straightforward job like bombing your house for fleas you can telephone an exterminator, explain the problem, answer a few questions, and get a ball-park estimate over the telephone.

Most exterminators will want to see the job before they give you a written estimate. They will and should make a complete inspection of your house. You are paying for their expertise in finding the pests' nesting areas and entry into your house. You can spray bug killer around just as well as they can, but the exterminator should know where to spray for best effect. He also has much more powerful chemicals at his disposal with which to combat the problem. Insist on a complete inspection before any course of action is decided on.

If you have a termite inspection done, make sure the inspector actually goes into all accessible areas. Termites, if left undetected for a long period of time, can damage your house severely. If the termite inspector cannot get into an area to make an inspection, then make sure that he or she makes a list of all these areas. Areas that can't be inspected should be treated for termites from the outside just to be on the safe side.

Before you agree to any plan of action, find out exactly what type of pesticide the exterminator plans to use and how it will be dispensed. The Environmental Protection Agency (EPA) registers and tests pesticides and publishes a list of registered and approved ones. Insist that the exterminator shows you proof that only registered pesticides are used. Also ask him or her how these chemicals will affect the members of your household, including your pets. Also ask how the exterminator will apply the pesticides. How much damage will be done to the walls, woodwork, cabinets, and other areas of the house? Who will make repairs if any are required? Will the house have to be empty? For how long? Will food, dishes, silverware, pots, and pans have to be removed from cupboards?

After the inspection, the exterminator will give you a written estimate. It should state exactly what will be done, how many visits are to be made, and how the work is guaranteed and for how long.

Guarantees are getting shorter and shorter. Most companies will offer a guarantee typically for three months for a flea bombing and one year for termites. Most offer a service contract under which they make scheduled visits; should you have a reinfestation between visits they will come back at no additional charge. Consider this type of agreement if you have pets that go outdoors. In many parts of the country it's just about impossible to keep ticks and fleas off pets that go outside. These pests come inside on your pet and set up housekeeping. Regular maintenance is the only guarantee against a reinfestation.

Some exterminators will deal with large pests like squirrels, raccoons, and bats; others will not. If you have such problems, contact your local humane society. They might be able to provide you with traps or suggest a person who will get rid of the pests without resorting to poisons.

CHIMNEY SWEEPS

Chimney sweeps have been around for centuries and are making a big comeback with the resurgence of wood-burning stoves and fireplaces. These specialists have the equipment and training to clean your chimney efficiently of potentially harmful buildups of creosote and other byproducts of burning wood. Creosote is a highly combustible deposit that forms when gases in the smoke condense on the chimney walls. If left to accumulate, creosote can cause a fire within the chimney. Soot is another problem. A periodic cleaning of the chimney by a sweep will give you the assurance that your chimney is creosote- and soot-free. Chimney sweeps also can perform maintenance on wood-burning stoves and fireplaces. Yearly removal of excess creosote and soot and the renewal of the door gaskets in a wood stove will keep it operating at peak efficiency.

Chimney sweeps can be independent entrepreneurs or employees of a chimney cleaning company. Many of these companies can also reline, repair, and restore chimneys and add chimney or rain caps. If you have a problem with animals in your chimney, they can install a screen to keep them out.

Chimney sweeps advertise in local newspapers and are listed in the Yellow Pages. You can also get a recommendation from stores that sell stoves and fireplaces. Most of these places have installers who are also chimney sweeps. These people usually do chimney cleaning as a side job when they are not busy installing stoves, so the summer months are a good time to get them to work on your chimney.

Most municipalities require chimney sweeps to have a business license but do not regulate them directly. Many are self-taught or have worked for an experienced chimney sweep. There are also schools and correspondence courses that teach this skill. Experience is probably the most important factor in evaluating the competence of a chimney sweep. If you are hiring a chimney sweep, you don't have to be too concerned about his vast technical knowledge. The job is not difficult if you have the right tools. You should check to see that the sweep has liability insurance and can show you proof of it. He will be climbing up on your roof, so protect yourself from potential liability.

Other work, like repairing loose bricks or cracks, or relining a chimney, requires more experience and expertise. You should be very concerned with the qualifications of anyone you hire to inspect, repair, or reline your chimney. Most of this structural work requires a building permit. See that the chimney sweep or mason gets the proper permits to assure you that someone else, like the building inspector, also thinks the chimney is safe to use.

There are contractors who specialize in relining chimneys and have specialized equipment to do the job quickly, and usually more economically, than a mason. If you hire one of these contractors, insist that he get a building permit to ensure that the work will meet all of the local building codes.

This type of work is usually bid on a labor-and-materials basis. The contractor should present a written estimate detailing exactly what has to be done to the chimney. If the chimney is outside the house, you might consider getting a bid from a mason to rebuild it and compare the two. If the chimney is inside the house, you will have to tear the place apart to rebuild the chimney, so relining it is your best bet.

Longevity in this business is one benchmark of reliability; affiliation with a manufacturer or distributor is another. You can also check with the Better Business Bureau in your community to see if there are any complaints against the contractor.

Chimney sweeps usually charge a flat fee for cleaning a chimney. This involves sealing off the fireplace hearth to prevent soot from getting into the house. If the chimney is for a wood stove, the stovepipe will be disassembled and taken outside. There is a potential for a disaster if the sweep does not contain the soot. Make sure that the written agreement or proposal that the sweep presents contains a clause stating that all your property will be protected from damage. The problem with this type of agreement is that it depends on who stands behind it. If the sweep messes up and your new white rug has a big black spot on it, he or she might not have the $5,000 to replace it. The sweep's insurance might cover it, or your homeowner's insurance might, but you could be left with no recourse but to sue the sweep. If he or she does not have sufficient assets, the lawsuit will not get you a new rug.

DECK AND SIDING CLEANERS

High-pressure power washers are an economical way to clean large surfaces. This technology, developed to clean large commercial buildings and trucks, has found its way to the residential market. Weathered wood siding and decking, brick, and masonry can now be cleaned quickly using various cleaning agents—chemicals, soap and water, and plain water.

Pressure washing will remove most paint that has been oxidized by the sun. This chalky residue will come off on your fingers if you rub them over the worn-out paint. Along with the chalk the water will blast off most of the peeling paint as it cleans the wood or aluminum siding. The high-pressure stream will also lift dirt and mildew from weathered wood decking. Because the machinery is small and portable, it can be moved around the jobsite. It's even possible to power wash a three-story house with a long section of extension hose.

Most jobs are figured by the square foot and the condition of what's being cleaned. Whatever you want cleaned should first be inspected by the contractors. Once they have seen the siding, deck, or other area, they can give you an estimate. A simple job like power washing a twelve-by-twenty-foot deck will run about $150, which includes an application of mildew retardant chemical after the cleaning. There are many cost variables and it is the contractor's experience that should determine the best approach.

Make sure you understand exactly what the contractors plan to do. Find out if they have a license and what equipment will be used. Will plain water or detergents be used? If detergents are used, are they toxic? Will they hurt the lawn, shrubs, pets? How long will the cleaning take? How soon can the deck be used or the siding painted after the cleaning?

If you are having a deck or natural wood siding cleaned, find out what you can do after the area is dry to extend its life. Most contractors will recommend sealers and stains to help keep the wood clean. They will apply these products for an additional charge.

High-pressure water will do wonders to lift off years of grime but it cannot perform miracles. Don't expect your deck or siding to look brand new even though the contractor says it will. Pressure washing will loosen rotten wood and old caulk and expose bad areas that you probably did not know were there, so be prepared for a surprise or two. If you have very old wood shingle siding or old brick, ask if the contractor has power washed similar siding. You don't want the cleaning process to result in extensive damage to the siding or brick work.

Long before power washers came on the scene, there were siding washing services. This is an alternative to consider if you're worried about damage. This custom cleaning service is done strictly by hand, making it a safe, guaranteed way to keep your siding intact. The contractor charges by the square foot; the job is usually more expensive than power washing because of the extra labor involved.

There is not much you can do to work with these contractors. However, operating the equipment is not too tricky, so you might consider renting high-pressure equipment and doing the cleaning yourself. The machines are available for rent at most large rental centers and some home centers. Rental fees vary with the location, but you should be able to rent one for less than $20 a day.

ASPHALT DRIVEWAY SEALERS

Asphalt driveways last almost indefinitely if they are properly maintained. Asphalt sealing is big business, but when it gets down to residential neighborhoods, there are many small companies operating out of the trunk of a car. These companies can do excellent work at downright cheap prices, but you get what you pay for. Asphalt sealing is known to be an area where ripoff contractors operate.

The best way to find an asphalt driveway sealer is through a direct referral or the Yellow Pages. Many paving contractors who lay out residential driveways also offer the service of sealing driveways. When evaluating paving contractors, be concerned with their reputations and how long they have been in business.

This is a relatively inexpensive project—a typical 450-square-foot driveway costs about $50 to seal. If you can't get a contractor to submit a written estimate, make him walk around the driveway and point out what will be done. Cracks and potholes should be patched before sealing and the contractor should explain the type of sealer used, how it will be applied, how long it will take to harden, and how long you can expect it to last.

The project will shut down access to the driveway, which means cars must park on the street while the asphalt sealer hardens.

If you want to get involved, you can remove weeds along the sides of the driveway. Cut the grass next to the driveway and use a lawn edger to trim away the grass that overlaps the asphalt. This will make it easier to apply the sealer and give a nice, clean edge around the drive.

BATHTUB/SINK/TILE REFINISHERS

Whether it's an old rusted bathtub, a chipped pedestal sink or ceramic wall tile that's dull and scratched, you can have these refinished without the expense of replacing them. Porcelain repair and tub refinishing contractors can refinish a typical porcelain or fiberglass bathtub for under $300. Minor chips and repairs can be fixed with a basic service call of about $20 plus an hourly rate of about $35. The words *refinish, reglaze,* and *resurface* are used interchangeably and involve etching the surface, bonding the surface, and then spray painting with a two-part primer and a two-part top coat.

You can also use this service to change colors in a bathroom. A vanity or faux marble laminate countertop that's not to your liking can be refinished in a new color. The contractors are able to match any color because they mix and blend the colors on the job.

If you have a fixture that needs refinishing, you'll find advertisements for this service in local newspapers, but by and large, the best source is a personal referral from someone who has had the work done and is satisfied with the results. If you don't know anyone who can recommend a particular refinishing contractor, check with a distributor of tubs and plumbing fixtures. These fixtures are often chipped during installation and the firms regularly employ refinishers. If you call a refinisher from an advertisement, make sure you ask for references and follow up by calling. Ask how long ago the surface was refinished and how the work is holding up. Also check to see that the refinisher has a license.

A minor chip takes a minimum of four hours to repair and a day for the coating to cure. If refinishing is being performed on your one and only bathtub, make outside bathing arrangements. Refinishing a tub is not an overnight transformation. A bathtub takes 72 hours from start to finish. One day is spent preparing the tub, removing fixtures, taping and masking off areas within shot of the spray gun, and applying the coating. On the second day the tape and masking paper are removed, new caulk is applied, and the fixtures are reinstalled. Day three is needed for the new surface to harden.

We have used these services with varying degrees of satisfaction. Our first choice would be to replace an old or damaged fixture. However, the cost of removing a tub sitting in a perfectly good tile wall is usually so high that refinishing is the only economical alternative. If the repairs are done right, the results are excellent. We had chips in porcelain repaired and we can't find the area after four years. We also had a tub refinished and the coating bubbled up, as we mentioned earlier in the book, and the job was a complete failure.

It has been our experience that you should deal only with established firms that can show you proof of a successful track record. All refinishing firms offer a guarantee. If you do your homework and find an established firm that values its reputation, you will get a good job. A guarantee is not worth the paper it is written on if the firm does not stand behind it. Check with your local Chamber of Commerce or Better Business Bureau for complaints before you sign a contract.

Index